MOTHER
GOD

Also by Sylvia Browne

The **Journey of the Soul** Series
(available individually or in a boxed set):

God, Creation, and Tools for Life (Book 1)
Soul's Perfection (Book 2)
The Nature of Good and Evil (Book 3)

Audio Programs
Angels and Spirit Guides
Healing Your Body, Mind, and Soul
Life on the Other Side (audio book)
Making Contact with the Other Side
Meditations (also available as a CD program)
The Other Side of Life
Prayers (also available as a CD program)
Sylvia Browne's Book of Angels
(also available as a CD program)
Sylvia Browne's Tools for Life

and . . . _The Sylvia Browne Newsletter_
(bimonthly)

☙❧ ☙❧ ☙❧

The above titles are available at your local
bookstore and/or by visiting
Hay House USA: www.**hayhouse.com**
Hay House Australia: **www.hayhouse.com.au**
Hay House UK: **www.hayhouse.co.uk**
Hay House South Africa: **orders@psdprom.co.za**

MOTHER GOD

THE FEMININE PRINCIPLE TO OUR CREATOR

SYLVIA BROWNE

HAY HOUSE, INC.
Carlsbad, California
London • Sydney • Johannesburg
Vancouver • Hong Kong

Published and distributed in the United States by: Hay House, Inc., P.O. Box 5100, Carlsbad, CA 92018-5100 • *Phone:* (760) 431-7695 or (800) 654-5126 • *Fax:* (760) 431-6948 or (800) 650-5115 • www.hayhouse.com • *Published and distributed in Australia by:* Hay House Australia, Ltd., 18/36 Ralph St., Alexandria NSW 2015 • *Phone:* 612-9669-4299 • *Fax:* 612-9669-4144 • www.hayhouse.com.au • *Published and distributed in the United Kingdom by:* Hay House UK, Ltd. • Unit 62, Canalot Studios • 222 Kensal Rd., London W10 5BN • *Phone:* 44-20-8962-1230 • *Fax:* 44-20-8962-1239 • www.hayhouse.co.uk • *Published and distributed in the Republic of South Africa by:* Hay House SA (Pty), Ltd., P.O. Box 990, Witkoppen 2068 • *Phone/Fax:* 2711-7012233 • orders@psdprom.co.za • *Distributed in Canada by:* Raincoast • 9050 Shaughnessy St., Vancouver, B.C. V6P 6E5 • *Phone:* (604) 323-7100 • *Fax:* (604) 323-2600

Editorial supervision: Jill Kramer • *Freelance project editor:* Gail Fink
Design: Amy Gingery • *Interior illustrations:* Christina Simonds

Library of Congress Cataloging-in-Publication Data

Browne, Sylvia.
  Mother God : the feminine principle to our Creator / Sylvia Browne.
    p. cm.
  ISBN 1-4019-0309-6
  1. Femininity of God. 2. God—Motherhood. 3. Goddesses. I. Title.
  BL215.5.B76 2004
  202'.114—dc22
                              2003018698

ISBN 1-4019-0309-6

07 06 05 04   5 4 3 2
1st printing, January 2004
2nd printing, February 2004

Printed in the United States of America

To my family:
Chris and Paul, Angelia,
Willy, and Jeffrey

Contents

INTRODUCTION

While I was at a book signing not long ago, a woman came up to me with my *Sylvia Browne's Book of Angels* in her hand. Out of the blue, she said, "I wish you'd write about the Mother God, Sylvia." Later that same week, while I was doing readings for two different people, each of them—completely out of context—said, "Why don't you tell us more about the Mother God?" My grandmother used to say, "If you get three messages, listen."

Although people have constantly asked me about the feminine principle over the years, the questions have never been as adamant as they seem to have been lately. So I said to myself, "This is the time. Mother God has to come forward and be accepted as the co-Creator that She is."

Further confirmation came to me shortly thereafter. One day as I was right in the middle of writing this book, my assistant turned on the TV, I was about to ask her to turn down the volume when I heard that Turkey had just uncovered a temple to the goddess Fortuna. "Okay," I said to myself and to God, "I get it. The Mother God who has prevailed throughout human history can no longer be denied."

If you've read some of my other books, such as the ones in the *Journey of the Soul* series, you're probably already aware of the Gnostic Christian belief in the Mother God. From the earliest recorded times, there's been a counterpart to the male Creator. In some religions, the female was the prime Creator, and in many religions She was seen as a virgin who gave birth to a messiah or ruling god.

Many of my clients say that they're aware of Her but would like to have a more in-depth understanding. Their questions range from "Why didn't we hear about Her before?" to "If it's true, why has the information been hidden or just alluded to?" to "What does She do?" and "How does She fit into the life charts we wrote for ourselves before coming here from the Other Side?" In this book, I answer those questions and many more. I share with you my research findings, and I provide in-depth answers to questions raised in the thousands of letters I've gotten over the last 10 to 20 years.

Even though my church, the Society of Novus Spiritus (New Spirit), is a Christian society for spiritual awareness, I've always encouraged the reading of all the religious texts of all religions. I firmly believe what our Lord Jesus Christ said in His Essene and Gnostic belief: "Seek, and you shall find; knock, and it shall be opened to you" (Matthew 7:7). I have also always said, and will continue to say, that whatever you read or hear, take with you what you want and leave the rest.

When I started Novus Spiritus, my goals were not only to have people seek their own spirituality, but to give back to them the true, gentler Father God. I also wanted to resurrect the long-buried but very much present Mother God. I'm convinced that if you keep researching and studying as I have, you'll come to the same conclusions about Her existence and the divine, powerful, healing impact She can have on those who ask for Her help.

∽∽ ∽∽ ∽∽ ∽∽ ∽∽

Chapter One

EVIDENCE OF
THE FEMININE
PRINCIPLE

Throughout ancient history, in cultures all around the world, people believed in both male and female gods and goddesses. Yet, suddenly, the Mother God seemed to disappear. Did She ever really exist? Where did She go? And why is She making a comeback now?

To answer these questions, let's go back in history and come up to the present day to validate that Mother God has always been alive, as it were, and powerful in all parts of the world.

Gods and Goddesses of Ancient Times

Ancient cultures and some primitive cultures today recognize God as an energy rather than as a male or female being. There have been several words for this energy, such as *mana* in the South Sea Islands. The Arabs felt that *jinn* inhabited the landscape, while the Latin and Celtic peoples felt that there were spirits in ancient groves. Others recognize this energy as a presence, spirit, or unseen power all around us. Of course, the closest we can relate to it today is the "force" of *Star Wars* fame.

In *The Idea of the Holy,* published in 1917, German religious historian Rudolf Otto put forth the idea that this energy, or "numinous," was a mainstay to religion. He pointed out that the myths, stories, cave paintings, and carvings were the way in which ancient people expressed their belief in this force and related it to their everyday lives.

In *The Gnostic Apostle Thomas,* Chapter 26, "Experience of Oneness: An Aside," author Herbert Christian Merillat discusses the use of symbols in relation to the numinous. He wrote:

We can observe that certain symbols are used by many peoples to help give glimpses of the numinous, the divine, the unknowable powers beyond conscious human experience and control. And among the symbols through which they express themselves in religious systems are the patriarchal Father, the Mother Goddess, and the androgynous primal human.

Merillat's observations show that, whether in symbolic form or in reality, the themes of intellect, emotion, and the Christ consciousness are continually being repeated.

Father Wilhelm Schmidt, in his book *The Origin of the Idea of God,* first published in 1912, put forth the theory that ancient people had a primitive monotheism before they began worshiping many gods.

He suggests that they believed in one god, who was usually associated with the heavens. In fact, many African tribes today still believe in the concept of a "Sky God." The problem was, however, that humans couldn't associate with such a high and Supreme Being, so they created a pantheon of lesser gods to manage the necessities of everyday life, such as taking care of the crops (fertility god), the weather (storm god), and wars.

It's impossible to prove Father Schmidt's theory, of course, but he does offer food for thought on why there were so many gods in ancient times. His ideas also suggest a theory for modern times as well: Maybe the Father God is so supreme that people can't relate to Him. Could that be why modern people are falling away from religion and why the whole "God is dead" movement started?

Whether She has been called Sophia, the goddess of wisdom whose name is found throughout the Bible; Theodora, the fertility goddess described in *The Other Bible* (excerpts of ancient holy texts that were excluded from the Old and New Testaments); or Isis, Cybele, or any other name, the Mother God has been around for as long as humans have had a belief in God. She was around long before the belief in reincarnation was born out of the Egyptian religion. You can rightfully say that She has been around as long as the belief in angels. In the Apocryphon of John, She was recognized as the unmoved mover: "She wanted to bring forth a likeness out of Herself without the consent of the Spirit." The Apocryphon goes on to say that the persona of the male God did not approve, but She, without his consent, created anyway.

Now, this seems to me like more myth. God the female and God the male have to be perfect and certainly not quarrel. I only include this piece to show how many writings valiantly try to make Her the first Creator, which cannot be true. Whether you believe in God, Goddess, or both, they have always been and always will be. From their love came the Holy Spirit and, of course, the messenger Christ who was the emissary to show that we cannot divide the intellect from the emotion. I believe this is what our Lord meant when He said, "What therefore God hath joined together, let no man put asunder" (Matthew 19:6). I know we interpret this to mean marriage, but some of the early Aramaic bibles use this to mean that the female and male within each of us cannot be divided.

The Feminine Principle Rises in Prominence

With the advent of agriculture sometime after the Paleolithic period, the cult of the Mother God became the strongest because She was the goddess of fertility. The Great Mother became more powerful than the Sky God (or male counterpart) and remained so for centuries. Evidence of this is found in the artifacts of a naked, pregnant woman constantly dug up by archaeologists all over Europe, the Middle East, and India. These statues or artifacts represented the powerful Mother Goddess known as Inanna in ancient Sumer, Ishtar in Babylon, Anat in Canaan, Isis in Egypt, and Aphrodite in Greece.

We find the female principle in all the Polynesian cultures as well as the cultures of Africa, Asia, Europe, the Caribbean, and North America. That pretty much covers the whole world. Sedna was the female spirit of the Inuit people. She has been known as the goddess of the sea and mother of the ocean, just like the Mother Earth that we hear and read about.

The Assyrian and Babylonian cultures had Ishtar, the goddess of love and war, showing her as the activator. Even in the Aztec culture, where we hear a lot about Quetzalcoatl (the male, green-feathered, serpent creator God), they also had Teleoinan, whom they called the Mother of the Gods and who signified the heart of the world.

In the ancient Egyptian religion, Isis was the goddess of children and magic, and she was also called Stella Maris (Star of the Sea). It's interesting to note that in Catholicism the Virgin Mary was also called Stella Maris.

Inti was the male god of the Incas and was married to the female goddess Mama Quilla. They were considered co-creators of the Incan people. During eclipses, the Incas would make a noisy ruckus to distract whatever monster was trying to swallow Mama Quilla. Some believe that the royal family of the Incas was descended from Inti and Mama Quilla.

Native Americans worshiped many deities, but one of the most famous was Awonawilona, the creator god of the Zuni. Awonawilona is both male and female; you might even consider them twins. Two other Native American gods, Father Sky and Mother Earth, arose from the streams and mists that came from Awonawilona's body. Mother Earth had four wombs from which the creatures of the world were thought to arise.

The ancient Phoenicians had two primary female goddesses: Anat, the fertility goddess prayed to by barren women; and Astarte, the Phoenician Mother Goddess considered to either be the planet Venus or to dwell there. Astarte was one of the many gods mentioned in the Bible as being heathen, but as we will explore later, this was mostly a religionistic political maneuver.

In ancient Sumer, the main goddess was Inanna, the goddess of love and war. It's interesting to note that both Inanna and Ishtar were worshiped for love and war, both activating functions, but in most cultures war is more associated with the male gender, while love is more associated with the female.

Notice again that every culture who uses the Mother God sees Her as proactive. She creates, bears children, and intercepts or protects against evil. Sometimes She has been seen as Kali, the Hindu goddess of retribution and one of Shiva's wives, but She's not usually portrayed to be nearly as ferocious as the male God who seemed to play favorites and was given to every human emotion such as jealousy, spite, anger, and petulance. Regardless of which way you wish to believe, whether you choose a maternal or paternal God, I think it bears stating here that if God is all-perfect, loving, and omnipotent, how can He or She be filled with petty human emotion? This is not faith. It defies logic.

It's also interesting to note that many of the pagan gods seemed to be just who they were—they stayed within themselves and weren't very involved with humans. Nonetheless, humans kept offering sacrifices and petitioning the gods, hoping not to make them mad. In the pagan tradition, though, the female goddesses weren't that static. Isis, Theodora, Ishtar, and the others were always petitioned, whether for fertility, war, vengeance, or whatever man or woman needed.

It's true that the ancient cultures often had many gods, but when you sift through all the research, you usually get to one major male god such as Zeus (king of the Greek gods) and one major female god or goddess such as Hera (his sister and consort). Most of early humanity just couldn't seem to believe that one or two gods could do all the things that needed to be done or provide the necessary protection on this Earth plane

God of the Bible

Now enters the God of the Bible who, at the opposite end of the spectrum, seems to be very involved with humanity. He talks to Moses, Abraham, and David. At least in the biblical text, God the Father finally has a voice, but He still doesn't seem to be as active as the feminine principle.

With the advent of monotheism in the Judaic faith, we are constantly told in the Old Testament of the confusion of the Judaic people in worshiping Yahweh and many other gods. The Bible is filled with stories of Yahweh constantly having to prove that He was better than the other gods because the Jewish people worshiped not only Him, but other gods as well. At that time, the whole concept of God was being debated, since some of the Jewish people believed in Yahweh while others believed in El (both names for the one God), as well as worshiping the various gods of their conquerors.

Throughout that period, the Mother Goddess was one of the strongest of the gods worshiped by the early Judaic people, along with Yahweh, and many even believed She was His consort or wife.

It almost seems as if the Old Testament felt threatened by the female aspect of God, even though in Genesis, the most telling piece of information is the use of the word *us* in describing the creation of both male and female in the likeness of God: "Let us make man to our image and likeness" (Genesis 1:26). As a former English major, I can tell you that the "us" refers to *who* made humans, and it happens to be a plural pronoun, which means more than one. That being the case, could there have been a creation of life by both a Father and a Mother God? We see the creation of life every day in nature; it takes two to tango, so to speak. I don't think it's illogical to believe that both a male and a female created humankind in *their* likeness. So we see in Genesis that Mother God was either a part of God or co-created with God as a god or goddess unto Herself.

Eventually, the Bible shows that the Mother God was pushed out of favor by the patriarchal priests, but people still worshiped Her secretly and even put hidden symbols of Her in the temples and altars of the Jewish faith. In fact, when archaeologists excavated the site of Solomon's palace, they discovered evidence of a giant statue of Ashtoreth, the goddess of the Zidonians. They found not only the head of a woman, but many images of fertility goddesses as well. Quite amazing, since we never hear about any references to the female God in the Old Testament. We hear and read that when the Judaic people felt abandoned, they turned to the old gods and were admonished or killed for idolatry. I Kings 11:1–8 confirms Solomon's love for many women—his 700 wives, his 300 concubines, (boy, was he kept busy!), and how he worshiped Ashtoreth, the goddess of the Zidonians, and Milcom, the abomination of the Ammonites. He even built an altar for Chemosh, the abomination of Moab, and for Molech, the abomination of the children of Ammon. Considering the wives that Solomon had and his many children, his goddess worship seems to have worked.

The story goes on to report that God was angry with Solomon for petitioning these other gods in the sight of Jehovah. As an aside, we have to ask ourselves, if God has this kind of pettiness or jealousy, is He as perfect as we must believe He is?

The Mother God and Worldwide Religions

In talking about the influence of the Mother God and Her effect on various religions, we must not neglect the Islamic, Hindu, and Buddhist faiths, for by no means do Christianity and Judaism cover all the world's religious insights.

Islam

It is not well known in Western culture, but Muhammad, the prophet of the faith of Islam, actually put forth teachings that made women equal with men. At the time (A.D. 610–632), that was unheard of. In fact, some of his revelations dealt with women only. The one thing that Muhammad did not do, however, was to acknowledge a female god. Al-Lah, the supreme God of Islam, was believed to be the same God of the Christians and Jews, but in no way was He going to be usurped by any other god or goddess. The first "pillar" of Islam is the Shahadah, the Muslim profession of faith: "I bear witness that there is no God but Al-lah and I bear witness that Muhammad is His Messenger." The greatest sin in the Islamic faith is called *shirk* (idolatry), which means to give allegiance to material goods or to put trust in lesser beings (false gods).

Before Muhammad came on the scene, the Arabs worshiped many gods, including three main goddesses (al-Lat, al-Uzza, and Manat). The Arabs were very disorganized and were divided into many tribes that constantly warred among themselves. After Muhammad had his revelations, the Arab world became unified. Many speak of the Islamic faith as the faith of unity.

Later in their history, long after Muhammad's death, the patriarchy of the Islamic faith changed interpretations of the Koran (or Qur'an), undoing much of the equality given to women and making changes that last to this day. It's interesting to note that, of all the major religions of humankind, the faith of Islam is probably the most tolerant toward other religions. It recognizes prophets such as Jesus, and it includes Abraham and Ishmael as its forefathers.

Hinduism

The Hindus have long been advocates and believers in the feminine principle, and their religion is also one of the oldest. In her Web-based article called "Incarnations of the Mother Goddess" (**www.shobanarayan.com**), Shoba Narayan writes that the gods venerated by the Hindus include many goddesses. She describes four of the most important ones: Durga, the brave goddess who rode on a tiger and vanquished her foes; Kali, the fierce goddess who wears a garland of skeletons around her neck; Saraswati the learned; and Devima, the Mother Goddess of all Hindu gods, who is worshiped all over India.

Narayan goes on to say that Hindus venerate motherhood, as illustrated by the famous Sanskrit saying, "Mata, Pita, Guru, Bhagwan." It means "Mother, Father, Teacher, then God," and represents the ideal of putting one's mother above father, teacher, and God. She adds that this reverence for mothers is also illustrated in the *Ramayana*, Hinduism's most famous epic. According to Narayana, the story is set in motion because "Rama's stepmother, Queen Kaikeyi, banishes Rama to the forest so her own son can rule the kingdom. Rama, ever the dutiful son, takes this to heart and gives up kingdom, wealth, title, and power because Mother Kaikeyi said so." However, Narayana continues, despite their obvious respect for motherhood, the Hindus still promote "a patriarchal society where a son can cremate his parents but a daughter cannot; where a man performs most Hindu rituals while the wife stands by his side; where the father gives away the daughter while the mother stands sobbing behind a pillar." She concludes that, as in China, Hindu sons are more prized than daughters.

Buddhism

In the Buddhist faith, we have the Mother Goddess manifested in Kwan Yin, whose name means "she who hears the cries of the world." She goes by many other names as well, including "the Buddhist goddess of compassion." She is Kannon or Kanzeon in Japan, Quan Am in Vietnam, Kwan Seum Bosal in Korea, and Guan Shih Yin in China. There are various spellings in the United States, though Kwan Yin is often used because it's the easiest for Westerners to pronounce.

According to the Website **www.Beliefnet.com:**

> The best known of all Kwan Yin's many representations may be the "White-Robed Kwan Yin," often called the "Buddhist Madonna" because she resembles images of the Virgin Mary. Draped in a white cloak, she holds a rosary in one hand and a vase of healing salve in the other. In some versions, she holds a child.
>
> Her story began in India, where she was known, at the time of the Buddha, as Avalokitesvara, Sanskrit for "He who hears the world's cries." Avalokitesvara was a Buddhist *bodhisattva*—a person who delays his enlightenment to aid in the liberation of all beings— and his compassionate powers are expounded in Chapter 25 of the Lotus Sutra.
>
> In the fifth century, this Buddhist figure came to China, where he remained a man until the eighth century—and ultimately transformed into a woman named Kwan Yin. Many scholars believe this gender change was the result of blending with the "Queen Mother of the West,"

a beloved Taoist deity. In Tibet, he/she is known as Chenrezig, and the Dalai Lamas are considered to be human embodiments of the bodhisattva.

Many say that Kwan Yin, as the goddess of compassion, evokes the softer side of human nature, the innate softness and unconditional love that counterbalances the drive for competition and dominance. The legend of Kwan Yin says that her compassionate spirit will manifest in whatever cultural and psychological context is necessary to help relieve individual and collective human suffering. Many believe her growing popularity in America is a response to social needs [as well as a parallel interest in the Virgin Mary].

(Author's note in brackets)

Suppression of the Mother God

On and on the stories of the Mother God continue . . . throughout Rome, Greece, Ireland, India, China, and in every province and every country. Why has every culture had the female principle except for the continents of North America and parts of South America? Is it because these were the main areas targeted by missionaries? Like the angels that have prevaded every culture, Mother God was also part of every civilization—until some religions like Christianity tried to suppress Her.

There are several different theories about the suppression of goddess worship. Why did so many cultures go from polytheism to monotheism? How did this change occur? Let's examine this topic more closely.

One theory relates to missing portions of the Bible. We are positive that the Dead Sea Scrolls date or even pre-date the original biblical writings. When the original Bible went to press, the Dead Sea Scrolls were left out because they hadn't been discovered yet. In addition, if you read the King James version of the Bible, you're missing seven books from the Catholic Bible. In the third and fourth centuries, the Catholic church basically decided which books or religious writings would be included in the Bible and canonized them. Many books relating to reincarnation and the Mother God were destroyed by monks who felt these topics would detract from Christianity. Many people today feel that up to 41 additional books are lost or missing from the Bible, and that does not include the Dead Sea Scrolls. How can a truth that has sustained itself for more than 2,000 years not be a truth? The politics of religion has declared what's in the Bible today, and it's a testament to God that the missing written material survived in spite of religion trying to suppress it.

Here's another theory. History is written by the winners. It was also written, especially in ancient times, by those who could write—like St. Paul. When someone is in an elitist group among illiterates, who would deny or rebut that individual?

B. A. Robinson, in an article he wrote called "Goddess Worship: That Real 'Old Time Religion'?" (**www.religioustolerance.org/goddess.htm**) offers yet another theory. He says:

> Many academics believe that the suppression of Goddess worship in Western Europe occurred a few thousand years B.C.E., when the Indo-Europeans invaded Europe from the East. They brought with them some of the "refinements" of modern civilization: the horse, war, belief in male gods, exploitation of nature, knowledge of the male role in procreation, etc. Goddess worship was gradually combined with

worship of male Gods to produce a variety of Pagan religions, among the Greeks, Romans, Celts, etc. Author Leonard Shlain offers a fascinating alternative explanation. He proposed that the invention of writing "rewired the human brain, with profound consequences for culture." Making remarkable connections across a wide range of subjects including brain function, anthropology, history, and religion, Shlain argues that literacy reinforced the brain's linear, abstract, predominantly masculine left hemisphere at the expense of the holistic, iconic feminine right one. This shift upset the balance between men and women, initiating the disappearance of goddesses, the abhorrence of images, and, in literacy's early stages, the decline of women's political status. Patriarchy and misogyny followed.

Judaism, Christianity, and eventually Islam evolved in the Mideast and Europe. Robinson continues:

The Pagan religions were suppressed and the female principle was gradually driven out of religion. Women were reduced to a level inferior to men. The God, King, Priest, and Father replaced the Goddess, Queen, Priestess, and Mother. The role of women became restricted. A woman's testimony was not considered significant in Jewish courts; women were not allowed to speak in Christian churches; positions of authority in the church were limited to men. Young women are often portrayed in the Bible as possessions of their fathers. After marriage, they are generally viewed as possessions of their husbands.

It's interesting to note that most of the changes in religions have come from conquest. The Mother Goddess survived in Judaism for a long time simply because other nations kept conquering the Jews and bringing their religions with them. In Rome, the first emperor, Augustus, considered the goddess Cybele to be the supreme deity of the empire. Cybele was called the Magna Mater (Great Mother) and "Mother of all the Gods." The Latin term *Magna Dea* (Great Goddess) came to be applied fairly indiscriminately to all the great goddesses throughout the Roman Empire, and it has been claimed that Rome was on the verge of evolving a universal feminine monotheism until the advent of male-centered religions such as Mithraism and Christianity.

With the advent of cities and religious politics, not only was the Goddess defiled, but around A.D. 59, so-called Christians accused followers of the Goddess of belonging to the occult, eating babies, practicing atheism, living by debauchery, and committing incestuous acts. It became so confusing that no one knew who believed in what, or how or where to go. The early Christians bought into the politics of the time, but at the price of losing any female balance to their religion; as we'll see later, that created problems. They now had a male God and a male Son, so there wasn't any female influence.

So the female God seems to have gone into oblivion for a long time. Oh, little tidbits were given to women now and then. In A.D. 431, the Council of Ephesus named the Virgin Mary *Theotokos* (Mother of God). Later, a 17th-century nun, Maria of Agreda, wrote *The Mystical City of God,* but her book was banned because it suggested that the Holy Trinity was God, Jesus, and Mary. In other words, the role of women continued to be heavily restricted by the male hierarchy of the

Catholic church, who tried to stem the flow of belief in the female principle. Exactly how did they negate these religions and goddesses? By making women less than nothing.

Yes, we were given a few tokens here and there to appease a world that seemed to be lopsided by too much intellectual paternal power. But if we are intellect and emotion, whether we are male or female, why is it illogical to believe that God the Father has a consort? Why does that make any religion, even Christianity, less effective? If anything, showing Christ's love and elevation of women would make it richer and fuller in knowledge and grace.

The Changing Role of Women

In my research, I began to see, whether it was Joan of Arc or the vestal virgins of the great Oracle of Delphi (women who were used to tell the future to weary travelers in need of hope), that women as a whole had been pushed back and used or brought out when all else failed.

There were vague attempts to resurrect the Mother God—She appeared in the popular fictional work *Mists of Avalon,* written by Marion Zimmer Bradley in 1982, and there were allusions to Her in the Dead Sea Scrolls—but most of the time She was relegated to fiction or became some kind of sorceress who could be bad or good, but powerful. For 2,000 years, I feel She has waited until the world in its chaos was ready for Her kindness and even Her sword that could cut through the darkness of the world.

I by no means intend to make this sound sexist, because I also have a special love of all men and number many of them as my dearest friends, but I am also for truth and equality. Be aware, also, that women in this country weren't able to vote until 1920. Susan B. Anthony fought for this right, but she died at age 86 without ever seeing her dream come true—at least in her lifetime. I'm sure she smiled from the Other Side when it finally came to pass.

Going back to the ancient beginnings of religion, it's strange to note what a paradox the paternalistic society of religion can create when it comes into conflict with the maternal. A great example is the "virgin birth" concept. Many ancient religions had a messiah or messenger born of a virgin, and this same concept appears in the Bible. (There are other similarities between the Bible and ancient writings as well. The Babylonian religion described a great flood and the destruction of evil sites; the Bible has a great flood and the destruction of Sodom and Gomorrah.)

However, unlike ancient religions that accepted and embraced their female gods, the paternalistic religious writers did not want the mother of God to be a goddess herself, so they made Her a woman and decided that the woman who was chosen to give birth to a God-man could not have any sexual interaction with a male. This, they felt, would make Her unsuitable to be called the mother of a deity. Here we have the elevation of the male, but they could not let him degrade the so-called Divine Vessel, the female who carried the God-child. Here again we see Her elevated, only to be put aside or trampled in political quagmire.

Most women in the Bible were portrayed as wily and not to be trusted. Salome and Delilah, for example, were vilified. But it all started with Eve, who "made" Adam eat of the tree of knowledge.

I often ask myself, why didn't Adam have a mind of his own?

In all fairness, we have to look at the times and realize that much of this material was written in rebuttal to the Egyptians, Sumerians, Persians, and Babylonians, who all had female goddesses. Perhaps it seemed that the concept of one all-powerful Creator would be too difficult a concept for an illiterate people to digest. Or maybe humankind felt more comfortable with a static, faraway God. The only problem was that the god or gods in those times played favorites, were given to moods, and had human emotions such as vengeance and even petulance. An all-perfect God (male or female) could not, by logic, have these human failings, not if we are to believe that He or She is perfect, all-loving, and omnipotent.

We do see a few instances of strong women in the Old Testament, but most of the time they were meant to be obedient and seen but not heard. We see exceptions like Deborah, who was a great judge; Ruth, the wife of Boaz, whose royal family produced the house of David, of which Joseph was a direct descendant; and Esther, who saved her people.

Esther was one of the heroines of the Bible. She became a queen of Persia, never letting her king, Ahasuerus, know that she was a Jew. At that time, as always, the Jews were being persecuted. Not realizing that his queen was a Jew, the king's chief minister, Haman, an enemy of the Jews, convinced the king that the Jews were plotting to kill him, so the king decided to kill all the Jews. Mordecai, Esther's uncle and adopted father, learned of the plot and told Esther. He urged her to speak to the king and try to save their people, but law prevented anyone—even Esther—from approaching the king unless he requested their presence. Mordecai convinced Esther that she must approach the king, even under penalty of death, to save her people, so Esther asked all the Jewish people to fast for three days in her honor and then she would try to approach the king.

On the third day, Esther approached the king and found favor in his eyes. He told her that he would grant her any wish up to half his kingdom. Esther invited the king and Haman to a banquet in their honor, to be held the next day. Meanwhile, Haman was plotting to hang Mordecai.

The night before the banquet, the king could not sleep. He commanded his servant to bring before him the book of records, which contained a report that Mordecai had once thwarted a plot to kill the king but had never been rewarded for it. The king called for Haman and ordered him to take fine clothing and a horse to Mordecai, then to lead him through the city on horseback.

When it was time for the banquet, Esther told the king about Haman's plans to hang Mordecai. The king, incensed, hung Haman instead and gave the chief minister post to Mordecai. Unable to overturn his decree to kill all the Jews, the king told Mordecai to send out a new law saying that the Jews could protect themselves on the given day. The Jews armed themselves and killed many who tried to kill them, thereby saving themselves from extinction in Persia. Esther, throughout all this bloodshed, was torn between her love for her people and her love for the king. At the end, the king made her his most cherished queen and commended her for saving her people. Through all the plots and killing, Esther held fast. Due to her love and faithfulness to her people, she saved them from ultimate annihilation.

As we see from this beautiful story and many like it, the Bible didn't totally deride women. Women seemed to creep into not only the Old Testament but into other religious texts as well, and to come at a time when all seemed lost.

In the New Testament, we see the continuing existence of some goddesses. For example, in Acts 19:21–24, Paul adamantly wanted people to turn away from all other gods, especially the goddess Diana who had a temple at Ephesus and was worshiped by the people there. Verse 26 says that Paul persuaded many of the people to turn away, declaring that the gods and goddesses were not gods, but only statues and shrines made with human hands. In verse 27, Demetrius, a silversmith who made his living by making statues of the gods, defended Diana. He said that, because of Paul, his trade would come into disrepute, the temple of the great goddess Diana would become worthless, and she might even be deposed from her magnificence, even though the world worshiped her.

We can't necessarily blame Paul, who somehow felt that recognizing the feminine would take away from the Christ principle. I don't see how it could, for no other messenger elevated women as Christ did, so how could the concept of a Mother God go against Christian principles? The Bible is filled with references to women who were like disciples, who followed the apostles and aided them in all their needs. Not only did Christ elevate these women, along with Mary Magdalene, but his own mother was a great part of his life.

If you are a Bible student, you know about a very special incident showing that Christ's mother was the one who propelled him into his public life. This, of course, was the wedding feast of Cana (John 2:1–11), where the host ran out of wine. Jesus was reluctant to do anything about it until Mary, in true motherly fashion, intercepted, telling him, "They have no wine." He rebelled, saying his hour had not yet come, but his mother simply said to the servants, "Whatsoever he shall say to you, do ye." He capitulated, asked the servants to fill six nearby water pots with water, and turned the water into wine. Most theologians agree that while this doesn't seem to be one of his most glorious miracles, it certainly started him on the way to become the Messiah he was known to be.

This story also shows Mary's emotion for the feelings of humankind, as she even paid attention to details that might be ignored by the static omnipotence of God the Father. Was Mary a representation of the Goddess? In my belief she was. She came and showed humankind a gentler and kinder part of God. Not that God the Father by any means has any negative human qualities. We certainly see some in the Old Testament, but the writers had to make their God more powerful than the Egyptian, Sumerian, and Babylonian gods. Christ in his mercy and wisdom came to bring about the new law: a gentler, caring God who resided not only outside but inside all of us.

I also find it very telling that, at the time of Christ's death, he first called on his Father (Matthew 27:46) and then called on his mother to behold her son (John 19:26–27). Many theologians feel he was asking John the Beloved to take care of Mary, His mother. It really doesn't fit right, though, for him to talk to his Father and leave his mother—but he doesn't. He seems to be calling on Mother and Father God at the same time.

But going back to religious beliefs at this point in history, there were horrendous debates on whether Christ was part of God or only a messenger. The God who came out of all of this was just as vicious a taskmaster as the God of the Old Testament. It makes you sad to see Christ, this gentle man who brought love and elevated women with his teachings of love and kindness, only to have his followers turn so brutal.

The Mother God Returns

If you are now thoroughly confused, take heart, because you'll see as we travel through history with the rise and fall of the Goddess that She would not be put down. In Asia Minor, in all parts of Rome, and even in Jerusalem, the Goddess seemed to hold Her own in small sects throughout the whole known world. And strangely or ironically, She was resurrected by Christianity.

In 1945, an Arab peasant was digging for fertilizer near Nag Hammadi in Upper Egypt. He discovered an old earthenware jar, cracked it open with his pick, and found a dozen old, leather-bound papyrus books. These ancient manuscripts contained 52 texts, now known to be the long-lost Gnostic Gospels. They were translated and published in English as *The Nag Hammadi Library*. In one of the gospels, the Gospel of Mary, translated by James M. Robinson, we see Mary giving courage to the apostles, who were terrified to go forth and preach the gospel:

> They wept greatly saying, "How shall we go to the gentiles and preach the gospel of the kingdom of the Son of Man? If they did not spare him, how will they spare us?" Then Mary stood up, greeted them all, and said to her brethren, "Do not weep and do not grieve nor be irresolute, for His grace will be entirely with you and will protect you. But rather let us praise His greatness, for He has prepared us and made us into men." When Mary said this, she turned their hearts to the Good, and they began to discuss the words of the [Saviour].

Here we not only see the emotion of the female voice, but we also see her giving intellectual reasoning to go out and spread the words of kindness and love that our Lord was known for.

Also from *The Nag Hammadi Library* comes the Sophia of Jesus Christ, translated by Douglas Parrott. It says:

Then Bartholomew said to him: "How (is it that) he was designated in the Gospel 'Man' and 'Son of Man'? To which of them, then, is this Son related?" The Holy One said to him: "I want you to know that First Man is called 'Begetter, Self-perfected Mind.' He reflected with Great Sophia, his consort, and revealed his first-begotten, androgynous son. His male name is designated 'First Begetter, Son of God,' his female name, 'First Begettress Sophia, Mother of the Universe.' Some call her 'Love.' Now First-begotten is called 'Christ.' Since he has authority from his father, he created a multitude of angels without number for retinue from Spirit and Light."

In early Christian history, women were the ones who held a type of teaching study in their homes. This makes sense, since women have always been the hearth of the home, and children usually learned first about God at their mother's knee.

In England, the Isle of Avalon in Somerset has been the home of the Goddess. It has always been called a place of awesome beauty dedicated to the all-powerful Goddess.

In more recent history, the Blessed Mother or Mary appeared in 1858 at Lourdes to Bernadette Soubirous, a young peasant girl who was later canonized St. Bernadette.

In 1917, the Blessed Mother appeared at Fatima, Portugal, to three peasant children: Lucia dos Santos and her cousins Jacinta and Francisco Marto. Lucia, the eldest of the three, was sequestered in a convent, eventually joined the convent as a nun, and until her death never gave public interviews about the details told to her by the Blessed Mother.

Our Lady of Guadalupe was also very famous and appeared to many with messages of love and peace as She did at Lourdes and Fatima. It's interesting to note that She never calls herself Mary, but rather refers to Herself as the Mother of God. This gives us pause to contemplate and wonder if the whole of creation and religion has been interpreted correctly. Is She the counterpart of God the Father, or is She the prime Creator?

The one truth guarded by the Knights Templar was that there was a female God, but because of the paternal rule, revealing it could have been considered heresy and meant sudden death. Consider how many things that used to be heresy are now accepted as truth. Catholics used to believe that if you ate meat on Friday and died on Saturday, you went to hell. That changed. Galileo was thought to be a heretic because he believed that the earth was round. That certainly changed. Heresy means simply that you must believe what the leaders say, and don't think for yourself.

We really can't be too hard on religions, either. They survived by how many of the faithful they could cull and count as their followers. Tithing also played a large role; if you got more followers, you got more money and you could build bigger churches. It became a race to see who got the most the fastest. Martin Luther got fed up with the Catholic church selling indulgences (which helped people get to heaven), and thus the Lutheran church was born and Protestantism started. Henry VIII wanted a divorce and the Catholic church wouldn't sanction it; thus, the Anglican (Episcopalian) church was born.

Many have tried to resurrect the Mother God, but everyone who did was persecuted for it. Yet She will not be denied. Catholics were criticized for many years for having statues of saints, but in the last 100 years, women began to be canonized saints more than ever before. Teresa (known as the little flower), Joan of Arc, and Ann the mother of Mary are just a few examples. The Catholics did resurrect Mary, especially when they declared 1954 the "Marian Year," and Mary seemed to hit her pinnacle.

When I was in Turkey several years ago, I realized that the whole country was silently worshiping the goddess they call Anatole, the Mother Goddess. Even their rugs have a hidden meaning—many show a female with her hands on her hips or in some other position. While it appears to be only a design, it is a tribute to the Mother God. In Ankara, which was the last place Mary was reported to have been seen, the site of the viewing is revered as the sacred place of the Mother God.

In the 1980s, evidence of the Mother God's existence began to leak out with the books *Holy Blood, Holy Grail* and *The Messianic Legacy* by Michael Baigent, Henry Lincoln, and Richard Leigh; and even Elaine Pagel's *The Gnostic Gospels*. It seems, though, that every time She tried to rise up, the paternal society of religionistic rulers put Her down as a cult or New Age fad.

I'm sure some will feel that the Mother God is just some add-on to make that "New Age" moniker more occultist. I hate the term *New Age*. The Essene and Gnostic beliefs are some of the oldest in religions. Historically, Christ was an Essene, which is synonymous with Gnostic, which means "seeking after your own truths." That's why Christ's teachings flew in the face of the rigid religious beliefs of his time. How could this man gain such popularity among the masses? I'll tell you how: He elevated women, of whom Mary Magdalene was an example. He taught love, not dogma, and kindness toward all. The Golden Rule didn't go over with the religions of the day because it came with no fear; and without fear, the religions in power felt that not only would their riches fall off, but they would lose control of the masses.

It was unheard of for a man like Christ to defend a woman such as Mary Magdalene, who was supposed to be jaded and a harlot to boot. My spirit guide Francine (who has been with me all of my life, as yours has), says that Mary Magdalene was espoused to a Centurion but didn't know he was married. The Centurion's wife accused her of being a whore and she was to be stoned, until Christ stepped in and calmly said to the crowd, "He that is without sin among you, let him first cast a stone at her" (John 8:7). This was a precedent. No one had ever stood up for women, who before this time had only been like chattel to men—less than slaves.

The Mother God isn't "New Age." She's as old as written history. Literature tries to couch Her in a shrouded manner, and religion portrays Her as just an emotional feminine principle, but in each century or generation we see a female trying to rise up and give hope to humankind. We see Joan of Arc, who led the French into battle because her voices told her how to proceed. For her good deeds and her flawless conquests, she was put to death. (I wouldn't have been too popular then, either.) How could a young woman with no military knowledge know how to defeat the enemy just by hearing voices? She claimed over and over that her voices came from God. It seems they must have came from a reliable source or she wouldn't have been victorious. It was the ego of the political regime not to allow a woman to gain favor, no matter how right she may have been, which gave rise to the Inquisition, where at least seven million women were persecuted for being witches. The Inquisition was called the burning times and is a great black eye on a religion that's supposed to be loving, forgiving, and dispensing of grace.

Plain and Simple Logic

If all this research and evidence isn't enough to convince you of the Mother God's existence, let me try just one more approach: plain and simple logic. As I mentioned earlier in this chapter, it's interesting to note that in most of the 26 versions of the Bible, Genesis always states: "Let us make man in our own image according to our likeness. . . . So God created man in his own image, in the image of God he created him; male and female he created them" (Genesis 1:26–27). Who is the "us"? Why, if God was only a male principle, would a female human have been created? I find it hard to comprehend why believing in a female principle would fly in the face of any religious belief, especially Christianity, since Christ above all the messengers elevated women.

If we were made in the image and likeness of God, there had to be a female principle from which the female part of creation was made. We are really talking about God having two sides like we all do: intellect and emotion. We are made in the image and likeness of God, ergo male and female.

It is also interesting to note that every embryo starts out as female until later when the genitalia come down. Could it be that God is trying to show us that we shouldn't disregard the feminine principle?

If nothing else, the fact that the Mother God keeps showing up—rising and falling, but still surfacing in almost a universal consciousness—points to the logical conclusion that She exists.

A lot of the ancient writings mention Christ as the first messenger born out of the Father and Mother God coming together. I'm a Christian, but I cannot believe that we haven't had many messengers who brought love and peace to a world that seemed to be doomed by chaos like it is now.

Buddha gave his message of love, so did Muhammad and many more who are too numerous to mention. It's sad that out of all of this love, humans—in their zealousness or ego—seem to put words into these messengers' mouths. They speak of forgiveness, love, and compassion, and out of this, wars ensue.

It also doesn't seem to matter what the dogma is in a religion; it seems to gain its success by its truth and effectiveness. Well, that's what this is about. God is always effective, whether in a singular or plural form. It's each man's and woman's decision to see what is truth for us, what not only resonates righteousness, but how we perform for God to learn and how spiritually we can perform in our lives.

The Hebrew word *Shekinah* means "divine manifestation," and it's interesting to note that *Shekinah* is a feminine word in Hebrew. The more you delve into all religions—Protestant, Catholic, Judaic, or the many others—the more you find the Mother God there. So much so, in fact, that you wonder how man could have kept Her hidden. Did we simply not read? Did we not search? Did we just take someone's word for what we should believe? I think it's all of the above for all of us. I certainly had help from my spirit guide Francine, but her vocal musings did not prove it to me. Not that I doubted her, but as stubborn (or dare I say skeptical) as I can be, I had to have proof.

My large base of followers come from many religions. They seem to embrace the Mother God without any conflict. The following letter from a woman named Susan shows this.

Susan writes:

A very old family friend of my grand-mother's made sure that my younger sister and I knew the Golden Rule and knew that we had a guide from God watching us. This was all we needed to know about church. When I was 40, after being bap-tized into my husband's church (Episcopal), my mind and heart were grief-stricken about what I had done and what I should do. "When you are 55, you'll know," I was told by my spirit guide.

When I was 55, your book God, Cre-ation, and Tools for Life *was published. Chapter 14 ("Protection Against Psychic Attack") stuck with me. I had been sick for a few years, always falling, breaking my front tooth and nose, needing stitches, and having arthritis and watery eyes so bad I couldn't even read. And my doctors could find nothing wrong with me.*

In July 2001, I was still feeling so bad and only now piecing it together. Chapter 14 convinced me that it just might be my problem. I promised Mother God that I would work every day for Her if only I could be around for the rising of Atlantis (Earth is a passion of mine). I followed your instructions exactly. Within an hour, my body started filling with a warmth and glow. My body felt 40 again, and I couldn't sleep that night.

Religion through the ages has, more often than not, catered to itself rather than to the truth. Whether due to the politics of the time, the decreasing numbers of their congregations, or how much money they were able to bring in, religions were nothing if not expedient. Does this affect God? Of course it does. We get lost in man-made dogma. Even when you look at the Bible and see what Christ said, and then look at how man interpreted it, it becomes totally different. Christ taught us to love and be nonjudgmental; his words became judgment and bias. And where is it written that Christ said if you aren't a member of this religion or that religion, you won't go to heaven?

We, as seekers of truth, live by the word and not the interpretation of the word, even though it's been translated thousands of times (strangely, it's only been translated once in Aramaic by Lamsa, which I feel is the only true interpretation). But then you have the fundamentalists who wanted to put their interpretations on the Word and who are dangerous in any religious or spiritual setting. If your mind closes and you become a zealot, you are headed for occultism, which, as we all know, can lead to drinking Kool-Aid with Jim Jones.

On the other hand, if you accept Azna (what we call Mother God in my church) as a part of your life, She accepts you and comes to you in your need. *The Nag Hammadi Library* includes a section called "The Thunder, Perfect Mind," translated by George W. MacRae. I'm including parts of it to illustrate what I mean. (For those of you who want to read the entire text, which is very beautiful and enlightening, you can find it at **www.webcom.com/gnosis/naghamm/thunder.html**.)

The Thunder, Perfect Mind

(Translated by George W. MacRae)

I was sent forth from the power,
and I have come to those who reflect upon me,
and I have been found among those who seek
after me.
Look upon me, you who reflect upon me,
and you hearers, hear me.
You who are waiting for me, take me to
yourselves.
And do not banish me from your sight.
And do not make your voice hate me, nor
your hearing.
Do not be ignorant of me anywhere or
anytime. Be on your guard!
Do not be ignorant of me.

For I am the first and the last.
I am the honored one and the scorned one.
I am the whore and the holy one.
I am the wife and the virgin.
I am the mother and the daughter.

Then it goes on to say in poetic form that She is all things, showing Her emotion.

> *You who tell the truth about me, lie about me,*
> *and you who have lied about me, tell the*
> *truth about me.*
> *You who know me, be ignorant of me,*
> *and those who have not known me, let them*
> *know me.*

> *For I am knowledge and ignorance.*
> *I am shame and boldness.*
> *I am shameless; I am ashamed.*
> *I am strength and I am fear.*
> *I am war and peace.*
> *Give heed to me.*
> *I am the one who is disgraced and the great one.*

This is a fairly long piece from which I have taken only excerpts, but it gives you an idea that the Mother God is all things and embraces every emotion. I'll end with an excerpt that I feel says it all about our Mother God:

> *On the day when I am close to you, you are far*
> *away from me,*

and on the day when I am far away from you,
I am close to you.

Today, religion is still dominated by males, which is all the more reason to embrace Azna, the Mother God. We need to have a balance to help us in our everyday lives, and while I'm not a feminist, She is an activist, and we certainly need that in our world today for peace and enlightenment.

~~ ~~ ~~ ~~ ~~

Chapter Two

WHO IS
MOTHER GOD?

In some of my earlier books, I addressed the existence of a female God, but did not offer information on Her functions. How far can She go? What does She look like? Why and when can we call on Her, and what are Her guidelines?

Francine, the spirit guide who has been with me all of my 67 years, has always professed the Mother God's (Azna's) power. Long before this research started, Francine gave information about Azna to my ministers and our Gnostic congregation, through me, in trance sessions. Francine was naturally effusive in her praise about the Father God, but she also told us that if we were Gnostic Christians, we should share our knowledge about the Mother God and try to resurrect Her, as Christ would want us to do.

From the beginning of recorded history, the Mother God or Goddess has played a major part not only in creation, but also as the great interceptor. In fact, She takes on many different roles and appears to us in many different ways.

Elizabeth A. Johnson, SCJ, is a Distinguished Professor of Theology at Fordham University and the author of numerous books. In "A Theological Case for God-She" (*Commonweal* magazine, January 29, 1993), she states that the scriptures abound with female imagery of the Deity. She adds that there's no reason we can't use this imagery ourselves when we think about God. Johnson describes some of Azna's various roles and appearances, citing the following scriptural evidence:

> She is the giver of life who pervades the cosmos like a mother bird hovering over the primordial chaos (Genesis 1:2). She shelters those

in difficulty under Her wings (Psalm 17:8) and bears up the enslaved on Her great wings toward freedom (Exodus 19:4). Like a mother, She knits new life together in the womb (Psalm 139:13); like a midwife, She works deftly to bring about the new creation (Psalm 22:9–10); like a washerwoman, She scrubs away bloody stains of sin (Psalm 51:7). These and other such symbols invoke the exuberant, life-giving power of women.

Names for the Mother God

Just as God the Father is known by many names—Allah, Jehovah, Yahweh, God, Om, Father, and a few more—names for the Mother God number in the hundreds, depending on the culture, the country, or the need people have for Her at any given time.

She has more names than God the Father. She is known as the love goddess, the killer goddess, the retribution goddess, the protection goddess, and the fertility giver. She is known as Mary and as Aiysyt, the Mother Goddess of the Yakuts of Siberia who records every new birth in a golden book and brings our souls to Earth for birth. She is also called Pinga, the benevolent Inuit goddess who protects all living creatures. In Lithuania, She is Ausrine, the goddess of dawn. In Babylonia, She was Ereshkigal, the goddess of the underworld. As an aside, Mother God was known by the ancient Israelites as Asherah and was considered by many to be the bride of Yahweh. Isn't it amazing what time does to history, or vice versa?

So, what about the name Azna? Well, it sounds like Astarte of the Old Testament, but my spirit guide says Azna is the name She is known by on the Other Side. I don't think the name really matters, but for this time and writing, we'll use the name Azna or Mother God whenever we refer to Her.

A mother praying in a chapel for the life of her dying

Amaterasu, a Japanese sun goddess.

son saw a lady dressed in white and wearing a mantle. The lady put her hands out and said to the mother, "Go back to your son, he is fine," and surely he was. She says Mary visited her, and I'm convinced that She did. Here again, what does it matter what we call Her?

D. writes:

I was pregnant, and my ex-boyfriend was trying to bully me into getting an abortion. Since I'm Catholic (perhaps not in the strictest sense of the term), I stopped and prayed as I was passing the church and the beautiful statue of the Virgin Mary. I begged her to save my baby. Almost immediately I was full of peace and realized how ridiculous it was to let myself be bullied into doing the wrong thing. Now I have a beautiful daughter named Maria. Is petitioning Mary the same as praying to Azna?

Yes, D., petitioning Mary, Sophia, Asherah, or Azna is all the same, and your feeling of peace was your answer. No matter what happens, ask for help and then accept your feelings; they'll show you how She answers you.

A Multicultural Appearance

I'm often asked what Mother God looks like. We are told by Francine that on the Other Side where great Romanesque structures stand (refer to my book *Life on the Other Side*), there's a statue of Her that stands in a high rose garden. She holds a jeweled sword in Her hand. In stature, She seems to be what we might call a Rubenesque woman. She seems to transgress all races, creeds, and denominations. She has burnished reddish hair but has also appeared as Asian, black, Indian, Polynesian, and more.

The illustration on the next page shows Azna's multicultural appearance. I see Her as having features that would prompt anyone to say, "I can see myself in Her."

The following letter from Christine describes what so many people have seen—Azna on the Other Side, dressed beautifully and standing on a stage or in a garden.

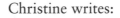

Christine writes:

Azna, as I see her.

I'm not sure if this experience was a dream or if I was really seeing Azna.

I was summoned to an area. When I got there, I saw a woman standing on an outdoor stage covered with roses. She was so beautiful that I don't think anyone can ever compare to Her. The scenery was gorgeous and extremely serene. The woman was dressed in a light, flowing, blue gown that seemed to be of fabric not of this world. She also wore a long blue veil attached to Her hair. She had the most beautiful smile on Her face, and She had Her arms stretched out toward the crowd of people surrounding the stage.

I didn't know who She was, but I knew that She was extremely important. Everyone was looking up to Her in anticipation of what She had to say. I don't remember Her words, but I do remember crying with joy and knowing that She was giving us the answers we'd been seeking. I truly felt that something extraordinary was happening, and I was very fortunate to be a part of it. I only wish I knew if it was for real or if it was a dream. I've had only one other dream of Her where I believed She wanted me to gather people for a reason that I couldn't remember upon waking up.

Also, when I was very little, I supposedly woke up and walked sleepily into a room where my parents were. Although I was extremely young, I told my parents that a beautiful angel had come to me and told me that I was born 200 years too early for a reason. My parents were shocked that I even had any of those words in my vocabulary. Since I don't remember this, I can't remember what the "beautiful angel" looked like. Could it have been Azna again?

Whether She appears as light- or dark-skinned, tall or full-figured, depending on what culture She ascribes to, Azna does appear. And She comes to us more often than any angel or spirit guide and to large bodies of people to give out Her message of hope, love, and even warning.

Azna and Her Sword

Many people write of having seen Azna with a sword. The sword is not a weapon or a tool to be used for doing harm, but a symbol of a crucifix as well as a device that can cut through negativity. She, more than anyone else, can wield that sword to cut away illness, negativity, pain, depression, and psychic attack (negative thoughts sent your way).

Brian writes:

> *I've been having some great experiences with Azna. I've been temporarily disabled for the past year with a severe concussion, a brain contusion, and bulging disks in my neck. I've been praying and meditating to be restored and healed. I saw Azna come from a white*

light. She slammed the tip of Her sword down, right in front of where I was sitting in a lotus position. She did this several times. White light was coming from Her, going in all directions. I could hear the clanging of a sword. After that, I went to lie down and I felt a heat-tingling-massaging sensation in the back of my head where my injury was. Azna said, "Stop taking your medicine; you are restored now." I did what She said, and I feel so much better, more energetic, and I haven't had seizures all week! Before this I was having seizures once a day. Thanks, Azna.

Azna Speaks

In *A History of God,* author Karen Armstrong writes that the masculine tenor of God-talk is particularly problematic in English. To illustrate this point, she relates that the Arabic word *al-Lah* (the supreme name for God) is grammatically masculine, while the word *al-Dhat* (the divine and inscrutable essence of God) is feminine. So, being emotion, it makes sense that Mother God would have more of a voice. (I can hear some of you wondering, *When didn't the female have a voice?*)

This next letter, as strange as it may seem, relates what many letters did—that the writer received real voice contact from Azna. That makes sense. Since the time of Moses and the prophets in the Bible, we've rarely heard about the voice of God the Father, but we have heard about Mary (or Azna) showing up in many places *with* a voice. It seems She not only appeared at Lourdes and Fátima, but to people all over the world.

C. D. D. writes:

> *My petition served as an affirmation from Mother Azna. It was a simple answer to a simple question, but one that startled me because I'd never heard of Azna and knew nothing of Her until two days after I received the answer while reading Sylvia's book* God, Creation, and Tools for Life.
>
> *I'd been contemplating why we were created. Upon lying down and closing my eyes, I heard a voice clearly state, "I'm Azna. I loved you so much, I asked God to create you." This was special in its simplicity*

and much less complicated than the visions
I receive.

The Great Activator

Let's look for a moment at the masculine force that is God the Father. He is all intellect as well as love, but He is very static. He is the unmoved mover, or *prima mobile.* Like intellect, He holds everything in place. Does that deny the fact that His power is everywhere and surrounds us, holds us, and forever loves us? Of course not. Never mistake the fact that He is very present. Francine says that in His power and magnificence, it's just harder for Him to hold a form for very long,

Azna, like the Father God, is omnipotent and everywhere at once. We are of a finite mind, so it's hard for us to even comprehend this, but I do know that when devotion is given to Her, She comes back with love and protection a hundred-fold. The Mother God is also all emotion and can bring about action. Because of this, more people have seen Her (as they've seen Jesus Christ) than God the Father.

There is no doubt that Azna is the great inter-ceptor. Being emotion, She can create miracles and can be used to dispel negativity. She has troops of angels who are always at Her side to help Her do this. Just as God the Father has dominion over His Principalities (his angels who, like Him, stand as protective sentinel figures), the Mother God has Her angels, the Thrones, who are more active, like She is. She also utilizes the other phyla of angels as well when needed. As I wrote in my *Book of Angels,* when the air-planes crashed into the World Trade Center on September 11, 2001, the Princi-palities stood around the crumbling tow-ers as power and protec-tion over evil, while Azna

Buku, a West African goddess and creator of all deities in that region.

and Her throngs of Thrones and other angels busily led departed souls to the Other Side.

In all of history, Azna has been the activator. In *The Cult of The Black Virgin,* author Ean Begg writes that with the advent of the patriarchy, the dethroning of the great goddesses occurred throughout the ancient world. Before She was demoted, the Sumerians recognized Inanna (Her ancient name) as a universal goddess of the heavens, fertility, war, justice, love, and healing. No matter what culture you examine, or how far back through time you go, you'll find the female principle as the heart, the activator, or the interceptor.

Even when I was in theology class in Catholic school, the priests and nuns described Mary (referring to the Blessed Mother) as an activator. They said that if God shuts the door on you, Mary opens the window. I always had a tremendous devotion to Mary, and in 1954 I submitted the following essay to the Marian Year essay contest (and won for best essay in the state of Missouri). What I'm saying now, and what I said back then, is that I don't think it matters what we call her, as long as we keep our minds open and try to see that there simply must be a feminine principle. It just makes sense.

FIRST PLACE MARIAN ESSAY

By Sylvia Shoemaker, '54

This year as the chimes sounded around the world welcoming in the New Year, many people bowed their heads and hoped this year would be different. They hoped to be free of the Communism and prejudice that threaten to corrupt our America. Exactly one hundred years ago a dogma of faith was proclaimed for all the world to know and believe. It was the dogma of the Immaculate Conception. Now we face bewilderment. We turn to Mary for the peace her mantle of everlasting protection can bestow on us, to lift up our hearts and pray; "O Mary, the voices of an entire nation ask for help and light to find the way back to you."

We look over the world and see Christ's teaching being trampled by the fast galloping horses of unrest and treason; and His words cannot be heard by the anguished people searching for truth. We see a world trying to fight lust, avarice, and materialism but with the wrong kind of ammunition.

What can any of us do we ask? Do we have an obligation as teenagers for we will someday be the ruling generation? What will we make of our world? What kind of parents will we be? These answers all lie within you as an individual as a free thinking citizen with a free will that God has bestowed upon you. This Marian year will be just like any other year, if we let it pass by unheeded. It will not be a success if we sit by and say let others do all the work, say the prayers, make the sacrifices. This year is a wonderful opportunity for us to mature into adults spiritually with the realization that we can help our nation and the world by turning to Mary now.

Are we now going to let the clock of time tick away every priceless moment of this year and see us no further along the way toward better world. We can some day be people of integrity or we can be sluggish parasites who feed upon communistic ideals and glorified materialism. So these hours are yours. This year is yours. Which is it going to be sacrifice and prayer for ourselves and people who are now on their way to everlasting darkness, or are we going to turn our backs? Before we do, we must ask ourselves, "Am I ready to see my God?"

SYLVIA (SHOEMAKER) BROWN

FIRST PLACE ESSAY

SENIOR·HIGH SCHOOL · '54

Chapter Three

PETITIONING AZNA
FOR HELP

Today in our culture of science, we're educated to relate to the world around us in terms of what we can hear, see, touch, or taste. We're not taught a lot about becoming more spiritual, nor are we taught about miracles or holy events, or even how to recognize them when they do occur. In other words, humankind's education is purely lacking when it comes to the works of God, especially in this day and age.

With all the research that's available, it's amazing to me that we, as searchers of truth, don't seek out and discover what an integral part of our life the Mother God can be. Even more important, with Her sword of righteousness, She can make life easier and make miracles an everyday occurrence.

Our church, Novus Spiritus (New Spirit), is now in its 18th year. Long before it became Novus Spiritus, it was the Nirvana Foundation, a research organization dedicated to ferreting out the theological truths of why we're here and where we're going. Eventually, the foundation made a natural transition into a religious society that began to have thousands of study groups all over the world.

When anything happens in our church, whether it's small or large or if we need help, we always petition Azna. While we never leave out the Christ consciousness or Father God, we turn to Azna as the miracle worker. When petitions come in, they're added to our "prayer line," which means that they're relayed to ministers who in turn contact their groups. Then everyone prays for the petitioners, usually at 9 o'clock at night. It's very much like Christ said: "Where two or three come together in my name . . ." (Matthew 18:20).

To tell you about all the miracles that have resulted from people putting their petitions on our prayer line would require a volume the size of a telephone book and more. We've received hundreds and hundreds of letters—far too many to put in one book—and they all show how powerful Azna is. As you'll see from some of the affidavits that follow, response to Her (and Her response to others) has been utterly amazing.

Azna's Healing Powers

Very often, people petition Azna for healing, either for themselves or for others. When we pray to Her, we all form a high network, not only on the Novus Spiritus prayer line, but just in petitioning Her individually (sometimes all day long). I'm often asked if She gets tired of hearing from us, but attributing characteristics like impatience or boredom to Her is just another example of trying to humanize God. No, She doesn't get tired. A perfect Father God or Mother God never gets impatient or aggravated.

The following letter is a powerful example of Azna's response to petitions for healing.

Nancy writes:

I am a novitiate and liaison with the Society of Novus Spiritus. I have shared this miracle with several of the ministers of Novus Spiritus, but I know I need to share my story for all to hear.

My grandson TJ, now five years old, was born with DiGeorge syndrome (which affects the immune system) and tetralogy of Fallot (a combination of four heart defects). TJ had open-heart surgery when he was six weeks old to repair the four defects in his heart.

We were told when TJ was born that he had approximately half the T cells of a "healthy" person. The doctors had hoped that his T-cell count would improve, as children usually acquire more T cells between birth and age two, but at two years of age, TJ still had the same number of T cells that he had when he was born. We were told not to expect any further improvement in his immune system, and for the next two years, TJ's T-cell count always remained the same. We were also told that because of his compromised immune system, TJ could not have any immunizations that contained a live virus. This could possibly affect his being able to attend school, not to mention that he could contract the very diseases that he could not be immunized against.

With such a low T-cell count, when TJ gets sick, even with common ear and throat infections or viruses, he usually has to be hospitalized to be given IV antibiotics to get him through the illness. I wrote a petition to Mother Azna asking her to intervene and help TJ so that his illnesses wouldn't always have to be treated by being admitted to the hospital. I also asked Her to help his body acquire additional T cells.

Mother Azna provided the miracle I petitioned Her for. During this past year, TJ has not had to be hospitalized, as the antibiotics have been working without having to be administered in heavier doses through IV. In November 2002, after TJ's six-month checkup, his doctor called to tell us that TJ's CD4 count had risen from 365 to 583, and his CD8 had gone from 169 to 500. His T-cell count is now within a range that allows him to receive all the immunizations he was not able to have. The doctor said they've never seen a case like TJ's. He said that very rarely some children beyond the age of two have had minimal increases, but they've never seen an increase this dramatic and will be documenting his case in the medical journals.

The ministers at Novus Spiritus have kept TJ on the prayer list for the past three years. There's absolutely no doubt in my mind that this was a miracle given to us by Mother Azna due to my petition to Her and the prayers of so many.

The True Healer

In this next letter from Greg, we get further verification of Azna's healing power, even when the person does not petition Her directly. Greg did not go to Azna for help; he came to me, and I called on Her. Whenever my ministers or I do a healing, we call on God the Father and the angels (especially the archangels), but we definitely ask Azna to send Her energy through us to the person we're attempting to heal. We can't take credit for healings because, after all, we're only the vehicles through which Azna's energy comes to the person.

Greg writes:

> *I was suffering from terrible back pains. Living and sleeping was a nightmare, and drugs didn't work. I prayed, because with all the doctors I'd seen, I knew healing had to come from a divine intervention. Enter Sylvia Browne. She was giving a lecture on spirituality, and after speaking for several hours, she looked at me and said that she had to do a healing on me. She came over and just laid her hands on me. I turned and looked at her, and felt I saw a direct opening to the Other Side! We hugged and I said, "Thank you, Sylvia."*

Three days passed, and I traveled from Seattle to San Francisco. I want you to know that I walked from Fisherman's Wharf through Chinatown to Market Street. (For those of you who don't know San Francisco, that's a considerable distance.) A miracle had taken place in my life. Just three months before, I couldn't even walk. Miracles do happen. Thank you, Father God, and also the divine Mother Azna.

I'm only including an incident involving myself because, as I stated before, I wasn't the one who caused this healing. I appreciate Greg's sweet gratitude, but he also realized that I was only the instrument. I'm not trying to be humble; it's just a fact. The energy utilized in this type of healing works because Azna wants us to know Her power and what She's capable of. You can do this yourself and have someone look at you and see the divine work of our Blessed Mother.

As an aside, I'd just like to add that it makes me crazy when I hear people charging money for healings or for teaching people to heal. I know we have to charge for services—I do because I have a huge organization to support—but I never charge for healing, nor do my ministers who do healings at our church services. Some illnesses are caused by cell memory from past lives, and they require extensive, time-consuming sessions with trained practitioners. We charge for those sessions, as well as for readings, but when we put our hands on top of someone's head and ask for Azna's energy to come through us and heal the person, how hard is that? The laying on of hands for a healing takes only a few minutes, and we don't charge for it.

Azna's Other Abilities

Healings are not the only reason to call on Azna. Francine says that Mother God is also very righteous, and if you call on Her when you're in danger of dark entities (evil entities that separated from God), She wields her sword to dispel them. That's why I've told people who feel they're under attack or in a terrible situation to ask Mother God to cut them loose with Her golden sword of righteousness.

Azna can also be very effective in helping you cut the cord from someone who's not good for you but to whom you feel addicted. She has also been known to help get rid of physical and chemical addictions by wielding Her sword to cut away the need for alcohol, drugs, and other addictive substances. And you can ask Her to intervene when you're worried about your family, friends, or spouse.

Please be aware that Azna will never do anything that will turn out badly for you. No matter how things may seem at the time, you'll recognize Her knowledge in hindsight. An example of this happened to me about a year and a half ago. My trusted husband found someone new on a trip to Egypt, and within a few weeks he was gone. He'd been my friend, my manager, my confidant, and my champion, and he was gone. I was flabbergasted, but in this instance I petitioned Azna *not* to bring him back, which was a temptation but wouldn't have been right for me.

As events unfolded, everyone began to come to me and tell me how he had tried to badmouth me out of jealousy. Jealousy of what? I guess my popularity, although I'd always felt we were in it together. The stories I heard later were hair-raising, but I never would have known unless he'd left (I've never been psychic about *me,* dammit). What if I'd gone on with this person, whom I can't condemn because I will always love what I remember? How much damage could have gone on financially, or with the people in the media who dealt with me and had their own horror stories to tell?

As this next letter shows, what hurts can heal. The surgeon's knife may seem cruel, but it cuts the abscess. The dentist causes pain when she pulls the bad tooth. It hurts for a while, but it heals, and life goes on, better than you knew it to be before.

Jack writes:

> *I'd just ended a relationship with a woman I was very much in love with. I begged and pleaded with Azna to please let her call me, write me, or just plain listen to me, but every time I made this request the answer came back with a resounding "No!" As time moved on, this devastation moved out of my mind, and I tried to move on with my life.*

One day I was sitting in my car, thinking about the situation and how much I had grown from it. I heard a voice say, "I'm glad you're feeling better, because I'm preparing you for something."

That night I got a phone call from a mutual "best" friend of both mine and my ex's. She said that she didn't want to be friends with me anymore because of the "whole situation." I listened and then hung up. I asked Azna why this and why now. The only answer I got was that it was for my own good. Although my prayer didn't get answered in the way I wanted, Azna helped me realize that I didn't need my ex to have pride and value as a person. Sometimes when She says "no," it's simply because She knows what's best.

I do know this as an ethereal, moral, and spiritual issue: Be assured that no one escapes their ethical consequences, or karma, when they base their joy on the ravages of hurting another person, especially with unimaginable cruelty. Azna is righteous and takes care of everyone, but She has no problem dealing out karma—not as cruelty, but as a learning lesson.

What Do You Have to Lose?

Recently I was talking to a man on the phone, doing a reading for him. He said, "Sylvia, I was at one of your lectures and I didn't believe in any of this stuff, especially that Mother God concept." Then he went on to say that he was facing a horrendous situation. I can't describe it here because the integrity of the reading must remain intact, but take my word for it, the situation by any standards seemed impossible. I told him what I often tell people: "Even if you don't believe, what can it hurt?" He said, "Oh, what the hell," and that night he petitioned Azna. The next day, the whole impossible situation turned in his favor.

Even if you don't believe in miracles, try Her. As I've said, and as this next letter will show, you don't have to believe, and what do you have to lose? It's like Jesus said, "Blessed are they that have not seen and have believed" (John 20:29).

Well, I have no doubts about the belief that will occur after you try Her and see the results.

Although this letter is long, I included it not only because it's well written, but because even though K. initially didn't believe in God, she more or less said, "What the hell? What do I have to lose?" As you'll see, she had nothing to lose, but she gained a lot. Her letter revealed a lot of skepticism, yet that didn't seem to matter to Azna.

K. writes:

When I first started reading Sylvia's books and going to Novus Spiritus, I didn't believe there was a God. I believed in goodness and being kind and so on, but I couldn't quite picture a kind of nebulous God who was "everywhere," or a God with a long, flowing beard handing down judgments; or really any kind of God, much less a male and female God. I had doubts, so (I know this sounds awful) I decided to set up a test.

I have trouble walking, and I really wanted a scooter to get around on. But I also have an extremely limited income. Just *for the heck of it, though, I looked at various scooters, knowing I couldn't afford any of them, and I saw a dark blue Rascal 240 long-bed scooter that I really liked. These things cost about $3,000, and I knew there was no way I could afford one. I even called various charities, with no results.*

Sylvia says, "Ask, and be specific," so one day I thought I'd give it a try. Even though I felt foolish talking to the air, I said "Azna, I want a blue Rascal 240 long-bed scooter, and I want it free because I can't afford it. Oh, and by the way, I'm not going to do anything to help get it," figuring I'd already done all I could by calling places.

At that time, my daughter worked for a storage company. When the tenants skip out with rent owing on their units, the storage company takes the contents and sells them to recover their losses. Most of the stuff isn't worth much. About three months after I "talked" to Azna, the owner of the storage company said to my daughter,

"There are three units I've looked through and there's nothing I want , so the contents are going to be sold. Go look through them and help yourself to anything you want."
So she called me, and together we looked through the first unit, which contained just boxes and junk. Then we went to the second unit, and there, behind more boxes and junk was—you guessed it—the exact blue Rascal 240 long-bed scooter that I wanted. Azna not only got me the scooter I wanted, She got it to me in three months, and She got it to me for free!

At the time, my daughter and I lived in a small run-down apartment in a dangerous San Francisco neighborhood, with street gangs everywhere. It was noisy day and night, with the sounds of gunshots, fire engines, police cars, and heavy traffic going by—a really bad place. Unfortunately, San Francisco and the Bay Area at that time also had the tightest, most expensive housing market in the country. We had rent control, so our apartment was very cheap, and people thought we were

*lucky to have it. Even so, I'd been looking
for many, many months for another place,
but because of the economy, everything I
could afford was located in housing proj-
ects or slums. In other words, in the same
kind of place I was already living in.*

*In one of her books, Sylvia says that if
you're asking Azna for something, you
might as well ask for the biggest and best
you want. So I wrote a petition to Azna,
and as Sylvia said to do, I decided to ask
"for the moon." I wrote that I wanted a
two-bedroom apartment I could afford
(with my very low income) in the mountains, surrounded by trees, and I wanted it
to be on a cul-de-sac because I was tired of
all the traffic and noise. And I needed it
within the month.*

*One week later, I drove to a low-
income housing company located in Silicon
Valley and asked, yet again, if they had
anything. "Well," said the clerk, "we just
got a unit that recently came on the market.
I think you might like it, but it's a bit out
of the way." She gave me the address, I*

looked it up on a map, and I set off. As I was driving, I noticed I was heading toward the mountains surrounding Silicon Valley.

As I followed the map, I came to a charming little town up in the mountains. Maples and fir trees stood on either side of the road, and I soon made a left turn into a quiet cul-de-sac surrounding a tiny little park with giant palm trees and redwoods in it. There was my two-bedroom apartment, exactly as I had asked for, and it was listed as low-income housing that I could afford. It turned out to be in the only house like that in the whole area—a beautiful historical home built in the early 1900s that had been refurbished into modern apartments. We moved in!

When we moved, we left all of our furniture and most of our belongings behind, except for a mattress and mat to sleep on. Most of it was junk anyway, and we didn't want to bring it with us. All we had were boxes of clothes and some household items we had cleaned and gone through. Once again I said, "Azna, we need furniture, and

I want nice stuff, not like the junk we had. And by the way, I'm having trouble with the car. I need that fixed, too, and as you know, we have no money, so the operative word is FREE."

The place we moved to happened to be one of the most exclusive towns in Silicon Valley—I mean rich, rich, rich. The week we moved in, I thought I'd walk around and check the place out. I saw some literature about a local church and decided to drop by. The morning I walked in happened to be the one morning of the week that the church handed out bags of food, mostly to people who lived outside of the area. I met the outreach worker, told her my tale, and was apparently one of the very few low-income people actually living in the town. To make a long story short, she put a request in the local parish newsletter for furniture and household items, and I received beautiful tables, chairs, sofas dishes, and two bedroom sets. And the church paid for new brakes and a drive belt on my car. Thank you, Azna!

The more I talked to Azna and studied Sylvia's books, the more lots of little "coincidences" started to happen. For example, my daughter loved The Lord of the Rings *and really wanted the Burger King glasses set from the movie. But Burger King hadn't sold them for over a year, and there was no place to get them. One Sunday after a church service in which I'd casually mentioned in my mind that I wished I could get them for her, we went to a local thrift store. There on the shelves were the exact glasses she wanted, and we bought them!*

I want to mention a few things that I think are important. First, although these events were wonderful and spectacular, my life hasn't become all perfect. There always seems to be some bad with the good. For instance, my upstairs neighbors turned out to be noisy and bothersome. As Gilda Radner's character, Roseanne Roseannadanna, used to say, "There's always something." Troubles occur, problems happen, I still don't have a lot of money, and on and on. But the most important thing is that Azna exists, and spirit guides and angels will help me if I ask them to. When I'm being attacked by life, it's easy to forget that. (Although I never quite know what request Azna will grant, I'm still waiting for the $17 million.)

Second, I think giving and getting is a two-way street, no matter how poor someone is or how little they have. We never know when we're being Azna's conduit for someone else. My daughter's boss didn't know he was helping Azna get me a scooter, the clerk didn't know she was answering my prayers, etc. I did thank the church's outreach worker, so I guess she knows now. But basically, I think we have to give, too, no matter how little or in what way. We just never know what part we're playing in someone's life. I really want to tell people that when you help someone— I know this sounds corny—but really, truly, it's yourself you're helping.

Sylvia says small and large kindnesses are like beads on a necklace, and sometimes, especially when we're going through *life with our defenses up and feeling attacked, it's hard to keep a mind-set of helping here and there, with even just a kind word. At the end of the day, when I do give a part of myself to someone, even in a small way, the memory of it makes me feel good inside and helps me feel more balanced against any hurtful memories I might have.*

I thank Azna for all Her help.

I will tell you this. Once Azna is awakened in your consciousness, your life is never the same again. I don't mean in a bad way, but in a glorious, spiritual way. She seems to invade your being and bring you righteousness, peace, harmony, and a sense of protection and well-being. I've been around for 67 years, and I'm sure I couldn't have made it through some of the hell life has dealt me—the same as it has you—without Azna.

By all means, pray to God our Creator, but if you want fast action, call on Azna. I always say to people, don't just listen to me—try it. It certainly can't hurt to see what happens. I have no doubt that prayers are answered. It's true many times that the answer to a prayer doesn't come out the way you wanted it to, but in retrospect, it's always for the best. And more times than not, results are immediate.

Ask, and Be Specific

Now, I don't by any means want to make this sound like an esoteric, occult fast fix. All I can recommend is that you petition Father *and* Mother God, but when you talk to Her, be specific. Of course She is God and knows your heart, but it's almost as if your words give Her power or give Her the impetus to move Her to action. It goes without saying that you can never use any force, prayer, or petition for ill; it can only and forever be for the greater good. It does seem, though, that the more devotion you show Her, the more She seems to move toward you. That doesn't mean She plays favorites, but She seems to remain almost inert unless She's called upon, while God the Father always and continuously holds you protectively in the palm of His hand.

I once asked my guide Francine if praying to Azna is more effective than praying to the Father God. Her reply was, "Not necessarily, because Christ really prayed to God the Father." But notice that the Lord's Prayer was not only a petition to make us better, but to glorify our Creator; whereas all through antiquity, people went to the Mother God (whether they called her Isis, Theodora, or Sophia) for the miracle of fertility or in times of stress. In other words, they turned to the Mother, whether in deity form or in human form, because She's always been the one who seems to take action. Even on the battlefield, more times than not, a dying soldier will call out the name of his mother or call out "Mom." This, of course, makes sense; this is where the heart and feelings lie. Even the great actor John Barrymore, that tough, womanizing, two-fisted drinker, on his deathbed uttered this last word: *Mother*.

It seems almost too simplistic to incorporate this letter from Ellen, but it typifies the fact that Azna takes care of everyday problems as well as larger ones.

Ellen writes:

I talk to Mother Azna (out loud) all the time and ask for Her help with this or that. In finding things I've misplaced (such as my car keys, coffee cup, camera, etc.), She comes through every time. I'd been looking for my electric blower for several months, searching every feasible storage space again and again to no avail. Then, by sheer accident one morning while I was feeding my dogs on the patio, SOMETHING turned me completely around and made me take a long look under a cluttered table next to the barbeque. There amid the dust, cobwebs, and last fall's leaves was my electric blower. It was hardly recognizable, so it's no wonder I hadn't seen it during the many times I'd looked there before.

Gardening is my fondest hobby, and my garden is quite large (about 91 by 56 feet). Each spring, my ground-preparation routine is the same. I remove all the stakes, buckets, bean poles, large stones, and many weeds; transplant all volunteer flowers and herbs; spread fertilizer; and smooth out uneven areas for the rototiller. Each spring, my late husband would clean, adjust, and start the tiller and we'd take turns plowing the garden. Well, starting an eight-horsepower Snapper tiller that weighs about 150 pounds takes brute strength, and you must take care to yank the starter cord all the way out or the kickback could injure your shoulder.

Realizing that the entire job was mine now, I had a long, very verbal talk with Mother Azna as I walked around that machine, turning on the key, setting the choke, checking the spark plug and fuel line, wiping away the dust and cobwebs, and getting into starting position. All the time, I was telling Azna that I could pull that cord maybe six times at the most, and since I knew nothing about cleaning and adjusting that big Briggs and Stratton engine, I needed Her blessings and all the help She could muster up if we were going to get it started. I took the "starting stance"—left foot on the side of the *machine, right foot planted back and to the side, both hands firmly entwined around the starting handle, and as I quickly snapped the cord out, I said out loud, "Here we go, Azna!" Needless to say, the tiller not only started on the second crank, but she purred like a kitten in a dairy. I was absolutely flabbergasted! It was necessary to till through the plot at least three times in order to chop up all the organic matter and mix it in well, and each time the tiller started on the first or second crank and operated like a new machine. Oh, if I'd only known about Azna two years ago when I needed help with that killer tiller!*

Mother Azna protects my garden as well. When I discovered pesky moles burrowing through the squash, herbs, and root vegetables, I told Her I wanted these pests OUT of the garden and that I would not tolerate their damage any longer. The next morning, I noticed a trail of mole hills heading down the center path toward the edge of the garden. There's one stubborn mole, however, that causes problems at

times, but leaves his hills mostly along path-
ways because he's been ordered out of the
planted sections.

Finally, I was taking a shower one day
and thought how nice it would be to soak
my tired, soiled, "garden-stained" feet as I
showered and then scrubbed them up after-
ward. Well, my bathtub and its plumbing
are more than 25 years old, and the lever
that trips the plug so the tub will fill has
been clogged with rust for the last three
years. (I had tried unsuccessfully to find a
rubber tub stopper to fit.) Something urged
me to reach down and push that lever any-
way, and when I did, to my surprise it
flipped inward completely and the tub
began to fill with water.

Mother Azna is awesome! She knows
when I need Her, and She responds with-
out being asked. When I'm running late,
She holds that green traffic signal long
enough for me to drive through, or changes
the red ones to green as I approach, then
finds me the nearest parking space. She
calms me when I get frustrated with things

not going just right, and when I have a decision to make or I'm wrestling with a problem, She helps me rationalize each situation to its best result. I'm so happy that She has taken my hand and is walking step by step with me.

Only Azna Can Change Your Chart

Not only does Azna have the power to heal and protect, She is also the only one who can create miracles or modify your chart. You may be saying, "If my chart is written, then how can it be changed without causing a chain reaction among all the people who have written the chart with me?" Well, that's simply what a miracle is. It's an event that changes time and even space to create a better good without disrupting anything. Consider this: Would it not be plausible that you wrote in your chart that you would petition Azna to create what you feel to be a supernatural event? For argument's sake, could it also be possible for it to happen just so you would believe that She could intercede at a time when everything seemed to be at its worst and couldn't be changed?

In my own life, I've seen things turn in ways that I would never have believed possible. Was it a disruption of my chart, or was it a part of my chart? Who's to say that you didn't write this, too, in your chart so you'd see what Her power could do? Maybe in your chart you wrote: "When all else fails, I'll find out about the Mother God and my life will change."

This next letter from Elaine shows that even if it's not a great catastrophe, Azna answers any and all petitions. As I said, She can interfere with your chart, especially if it brings about a better good.

Elaine writes:

My brother (whose only son is living with my parents) and his wife were planning to come out to New Jersey today to buy a Harley-Davidson motorcycle that they saw on eBay. They owe my dad $5,000 for the divorce they never got when my brother wanted to leave because his wife had put him $3,000 in the hole writing bad checks.

All the employees in my sister-in-law's company were to receive a sum of money, and she and my brother were going to use hers to buy this "death" cycle. Then they were planning to spend the night in my one-room place. They both smoke like chimneys and would want me to go out to some loud, smoky place to drink, but I was supposed to sing in a concert in New York the next day. My parents always call on Saturday morning, and I was going to have a hard time explaining what those two were doing out here. The whole idea was giving me an ulcer, so I petitioned Azna that the deal would somehow fall through.

As it turns out, everyone at my sister-in-law's company received their checks but her, and the company swore it was sent out. The post office shrugged its shoulders, and nobody knew what happened to that check. My brother and sister-in-law were unable to spend that money on this foolishness and further upset the family. I slept in my own bed that night, got up when I was

ready, and took my time getting ready for
my performance.
    Praise to Azna! She listens and She acts!

Put It in Writing

Like Gnostics who have always believed in
writing letters to the universe, many people have
found that sitting down and writing out their petitions to Azna can be very helpful. In times of stress,
I often sit down and write out my petition, light a
white candle for the Holy Spirit, call on the Christ
consciousness and Father God, and then burn the
petition. This ritual has no mystical power except
what I put into it. It's like melding my will with
God's to bring about help, endurance, or even a
miracle.

Whenever you face a situation that seems insur-
mountable, Azna is the one you should go to. Follow the same steps I've outlined above, but call on
Mother God and She can help give you the answer,
even if it's only to sweep away the cobwebs of
your mind so you can make the right decision. So
often when I've petitioned Her in times of stress, a

word, thought, idea, or solution has come into my mind unbidden, so I knew for sure it hadn't come from me. Most of the time it was so simple that I wanted to slap my forehead in amazement.

This next letter is a beautiful example of what can happen when you write your petitions to Azna.

Amanda writes:

Like many, I too have a wonderful story to tell about our dear Mother. About three years ago, I was in great despair. After losing my mother and my grandfather in the span of two years, I was extremely depressed. One day, after reading Sylvia's book The Other Side and Back, *I decided to petition Azna for help.*

I wrote an extensive letter to Her, detailing everything that I wanted to go right in my life (one item was to battle my grief and despair). In this letter, I gave myself six months to a year for improvement. As I went through the year, I really didn't think much of the petition until one day when I was cleaning out my closets and saw the copy I'd made of the letter (I'd made two copies, burning one and saving the other). I quickly began to reread it and realized that everything I'd pleaded to Her had come true. I'd gotten into the college that I wanted to, I'd gained the self-esteem I desired to have, and my relationship with my fiancé, Harry, was back to normal and we were in love again for all the right reasons.

Not only had this relationship improved, but our finances had improved greatly. Harry kept getting raises left and right, and my dad kept sending us money just when we really needed it (and we never asked him for it—he just loved to send it up)! My grief from my mother and grandfather's passing had not disappeared, but it was more tolerable than it had been in the past.

I'm such a firm believer now in asking for what you want, because if your chart allows it, She will make it happen! This experience has greatly increased my spiritual strength. I don't write things off so quickly anymore as coincidence because I know there's a greater force out there assisting us at all times.

This happens often. We ask, time goes by, and we don't realize that what we've asked for has come true.

A Prayer to Azna

Aside from writing out your petitions, there's a very effective meditative prayer that you can use to ask for Azna's help, and I'm including it here as a final thought for this chapter.

Light a white candle and sit or lie in a comfortable position. I prefer to sit upright with my feet on the floor and my hands upward on my thighs so I can allow grace to come into my hands. Take three deep breaths and ask that the white light of the Holy Spirit come around you. Also ask that God the Father hold you in His hands and that the Christ consciousness come around you. Ask for the Thrones (Azna's special army of angels) to make a circle around you. Then say the following prayer:

Dearest Mother, I come to You with love and heartfelt adoration. I come with thanksgiving for all You have done for me, and I know You will continue to help me on this road of life. I come to You with many needs and know You will help me with swift accuracy. I need Your help with [insert petition]. *Please guide me in the best resolution to this problem. I need Your help if I am sick or* [insert problem]. *I need You to give me solace over a loss, whether it is due to death, divorce, or just a deception from a loved one. Help me get over the pain of any disappointment, sorrow, or dissension in my life so that I can find my true, happy, and well self and go on, not only to glorify Your name, but to help others in need.*

I ask this and any other petition I haven't thought of, so that with Your sword of justice, You can cut through depression, addiction, jealousy, deception, sorrow, greed, or any injustice that I have suffered. I want no harm to come to anyone, I just want to fulfill my chart and expect a miracle. I realize that no matter how large or small my petition is, it will be done for my better good and the good of all. Send me Your love and grace to carry me through each day, and keep Your sword and mantle ready to encompass me and keep all negativity from me. I ask this in Your name. Amen.

~~ ~~ ~~ ~~ ~~

Chapter Four

FREQUENTLY ASKED QUESTIONS

The following questions about Azna, or the Mother God, are just a few of the many that have been sent to me in letters, cards, and e-mails over the years.

Q. Why is Azna coming forward now rather than before?

I think it's because more and more women are beginning to search for the truth, instead of just being lazy and giving their souls over to what one person or group says. I think we're also researching more to find truth, and when we do this, we are truly Gnostic. Whether you accept the truth or not, God bless you for searching. If you don't search for truth, you leave your soul open to being filled with nothing but singular, man-made beliefs that many times have nothing to do with historical truth. I also think She's coming forward now because the world needs a more maternal side to civilization.

Q. Why do you describe Her with a sword?

My spirit guide Francine says that's Her symbol. As I stated earlier, the sword is also in the shape of a cross, for Christ consciousness. Mother God's sword is not for vengeance, but for Her ability to cut through negativity. It has a golden handle with a silver or platinum blade.

Q. Why does She change Her appearance?

Because She is the Mother God, She would be politically correct to appear as an Asian, a Caucasian, a Spaniard, and so on. Like us on the Other Side, She can take any visage She chooses. This certainly doesn't diminish Her power and ability.

Q. Why does She seem to send flowers?

Many years ago, my grandmother, Ada Coil, who was a great psychic in Kansas City, Missouri, explained to me about Mother God (she had learned from her mother). She said that when Mother God seems to send us flowers, it's like Her love letter to us, to show She's listening. Like a love note sent back, it can come in the strangest ways. When you ask for Her response, give Her a time limit. One time I asked, "In seven or ten days, let me receive a flower." About seven days later, a little girl came up to me at our church and said, "I felt I had to give this to you." It was a yellow rose.

Q. How long has Mother God been around?

From the very beginning. If there is a God the Father who always was, there was also a Mother God. For that matter, there were also all of us. The Father and Mother Gods are perfect, so They just didn't decide one day to make Her or us. We all always were.

Q. What happens if we don't believe in Her?

It doesn't matter. Again, God is all-loving and perfect, so it's really our loss if we don't believe, but it certainly doesn't hurt Them. I just smile to myself and realize that when we get to the Other Side, the proof will be there.

However, I'm convinced that if you research, as I've stated over and over again, you'll find the same truths that I've found. You shouldn't depend on the words of one source, not even mine. Look and seek and find and you will uncover—as so many of us have—Azna still standing, maybe a little dusty from time, but still standing in all Her splendor, ready to assist you at any given moment.

Q. Do you ever get hate mail from religious groups for talking about the Mother God?

No, I don't. Why? I don't know, really, except that when people know you are dedicated to God and all His or Her messengers (in my case, Christ), what can they hate about you? I have always felt, though (and my ministry is clear on this), that I have tried to hold up a loving Christ and an all-knowing, loving God, male and female. This is the same thing that Christ did during his lifetime, even though it flew in the face of all the temples that were losing members and sealed his doom with the Jewish faith when he said, "The temple of God is within."

Q. Does She always help us?

Not always, but I will stand by this statement without reservation: More times than not, your prayers will be answered. Note that you can pray to Father God, but He is not the activator.

Q. Why is there even a Mother God?

Well, it makes sense that everything is in duality, male and female. To get even more basic, what were we females made in the likeness of? We even have a male and female side of our brain. So why not a female Creator?

Q. What does She do?

Rather, what *can't* She do? I've seen thousands of affidavits and letters over the years that prove that there is no category She can't address, from the very minute to the more serious issues, and Her intervention doesn't seem to interfere with our charts. Maybe we even wrote Her into our charts.

Q. Can She change our charts?

I have a feeling that She can modify our charts or cause a miracle to happen, or perhaps intervene in a chart that has gone awry or that we just can't stand.

Q. Can She create things?

She can't create what hasn't already been created. She just changes the circumstances around to create a better situation or a better outcome.

Q. Is She more powerful than Father God?

No, not at all. They are the same in power, just different facets of the same power. God the Father is static and holds us in place, as it were. Mother God is the great interceptor.

Q. How do I talk to Her?

You can pray to Her, but personally I think talking in your own words is just as good. After all, God knows everything, especially your intentions.

〜〜 〜〜 〜〜 〜〜 〜〜

Chapter Five

LETTERS AND STORIES ABOUT MOTHER GOD

When I wrote my book *Sylvia Browne's Book of Angels,* I put a request on my Website (**www.Sylvia.org**) asking for angel stories. The response was more than my office could handle, but even after that experience, no one on my staff was prepared for the unbelievable number of replies we received when I recently asked for stories about miracles related to Azna. The response was overwhelming. Thousands of e-mails poured in from everywhere. I've never been one for statistics, because anyone can make anything sound the way they it want to, but even *I* had to take a deep bow over the thousands of e-mails that came in.

After only a few days, we had to shut the site down because it was too much to handle. We all said that even the most hardened nonbelievers would feel something stir in their souls after seeing all of this. Whether they felt nothing more than a response to the poignant miracle stories, or perhaps a primordial truth coming alive from somewhere in their limbic brain (the old brain), there would be a stirring of the possibility that there is truth here.

We even got letters from skeptics who had called on Mother God as a test, and Her answers came to them. Apparently, the belief factor seems to have no bearing on what happens. I feel that She just wants people to know that Her power, with God the Father's power, can create miracles.

It is with this in mind that I now put forth a few letters regarding the power of Mother God.

❧❧❧

This first letter typifies the thousands of letters we received about the miracles of Mother God (Azna). So many were about health-related issues and Azna's wonderful intervention.

Darren writes:

I petitioned Mother Azna to help me with my health, specifically in regards to HIV. In the past two years, my T cells have gone from 5 to over 250, and my viral load has remained undetectable. I have the lab reports to back up what I'm saying.

அஇௐ அஇௐ அஇௐ

The next letter describes another health issue that seemed no less than desperate. Sandy writes:

Last July, I was 29 weeks pregnant when the placenta detached from the uterine wall (I knew this would happen, since I'd dreamed about the event seven years earlier). My baby, Conor, started down the canal—butt first. As I was preparing for an emergency C-section, I was experiencing thoughts not my own. I was told there were two options—one positive and one difficult—and the choice was mine. If I wanted Conor to be healthy, I needed to call out to Azna for help. I did, much to the surprise of everyone in the operating room. Although they said nothing, I had the clear impression that everyone in that room understood what had happened. Conor was born healthy at three pounds and came out breathing on his own. He was fully developed—a total surprise for the natal intensive-care staff.

Every fiber of my being knows Azna intervened, and I will always be grateful for Her help. Whenever I tell the story of Conor's birth, I always tell people it was because of Her that he is healthy today.

ஐ౿ ஐ౿ ஐ౿

The following story shows that even if Azna doesn't cure, She answers prayers. Lori writes:

Last July 1, I had to say yes to my granny's surgery. From that day on, I asked Mother Azna not to allow this beautiful, loving woman to suffer for months. Then I got a call for a job that I'd been trying to get for years. Every day and night, I took my prayer book and read it from beginning to end. Granny passed on July 25, and I had to start my new job four days later—the day my granny was buried. I was happy yet sad, grateful, and mad. You see, my dear granny didn't want me there; I would've been a basket case.

᪷᪷᪷ ᪷᪷᪷ ᪷᪷᪷

As the next four letters show, Azna has been known to give out flowers as a symbol of Her presence. I've tried this myself, and it works nine out of ten times. Try it. Ask your petition and then ask for a flower to come to you in a week. It will come in the most surprising ways. This means that Azna is listening. Your petition may not be answered exactly as you want, but a flower symbolizes that She's here always and listening.

Lynne writes:

A couple years ago, I read in one of Sylvia's books that Azna loves to send a flower via an unexpected source, showing that She's heard your petition. Well, I decided to try it. I prayed to Azna about a problem I was having and asked Her to send me a flower within one week so I'd know She'd heard my petition. About six days later I found a rose—the most perfect red rose I'd ever seen—in my mailbox. I was so excited because I felt in my soul that it had come from Azna.

Later that day, I found that the physical source of the flower was a friend of mine who worked at a flower shop. For some reason, the florist had a dozen red roses she had to get rid of. She asked my friend if he'd like to have them for someone. Well, my friend had no one to give a dozen roses to but thought I would like to have one of them and left it in my mailbox. Even though the rose came from my friend, it did come from an unexpected source—

the florist who wanted to unload a dozen roses.

I still have that rose. It was a large bud that never bloomed, and it dried to perfection. I call it my "Mother God rose."

꧁ ꧁ ꧁

Barbara writes:

The magic of Mother Azna's answer to my desperate petition on behalf of my dad changed my life forever. Last year my father was diagnosed with advanced lung cancer, and we spent most of 2002 shuffling back and forth from San Francisco to the M. D. Anderson Cancer Center in Houston, Texas.

My father's diagnosis came out of the blue. He had virtually no symptoms, and he only found out when I practically forced him to get a full body scan. This news was devastating to us all, and particularly to me, since I'd been working very hard on some personal core issues, one of them being that deep down I somehow felt responsible on a "spirit" level for keeping my father healthy. As strange as it sounds, I had a fundamental belief (one that took me a long time to recognize) that I had to sacrifice my own "life force" in order to keep him healthy and on this earth. Through a lot of soul searching, meditation, and prayer, I'd finally begun to free myself of this fundamental belief when we received the shocking news. At that point my father and I were both relatively healthy, and I'd begun to release the "cell level" belief.

When we got the news, I was so confused. It was as if the universe had finally convinced me that I could focus on my own health and no longer be that little girl waiting for the rug to pulled out from under her. And then suddenly—bam!—one of my worst fears became realized. I was confused, hurt, guilty, scared, and angry all at the same time.

When we began going back and forth to Houston, I started my journey with Sylvia Browne. Her books were the light that my spirit had been waiting for. Every-thing seemed familiar and right. The con-cept of Mother God was one that I innately knew to be true. I began to feel immense relief in the beautiful simplicity of it all, and I began to follow Sylvia and Francine's advice in petitioning Mother Azna to help with my dad's case. First, as they talked about in her books, I asked Mother Azna for a sign in the form of flowers that She indeed had heard my prayers. Sylvia stated that after I asked, I could expect to get a flower or flowers out of the blue within a short period of time.

When day three arrived and there were still no flowers, I resigned myself to the fact that things like that didn't happen to me. Then that evening, at an Italian restau-rant, the waiter came to take our dinner order. I already knew I was going to order a particular meat dish. However, when it was my turn to order, I heard coming out of my mouth (without knowing why), "I'll have the risotto with asparagus." I'd had no intention of ordering that, but I just assumed that, with the stress of our situation, I wasn't thinking straight. I didn't, however, change the order. When our meals arrived, to my sheer delight, mine was the only dish with a beautiful pink flower in the middle of the risotto! A peaceful calm came over me, and all I could do was smile in my immediate knowingness. At that moment, I realized that magic truly exists.

After that initial sign, I began having more and more. A day or two later I found a perfectly creased heart on my sheet when I pulled the covers down. No one had been in my hotel room that evening. The other bed didn't have one, nor did the bed in my parents' connecting room. Later that night, as I went to bed, I found another heart on the other side of the bed.

After five months of treatment (and a whole new life of magic for me, thanks to the remarkable work and boundless spirit of Sylvia Browne), we returned to Houston to hear the good news—my father's cancer was seemingly gone! And it has remained that way up to this point, eight months later.

෴ ෴ ෴

Sequim writes:

As I walked along the river with my dog, Sierra, I wondered aloud, "Okay, Azna, where's the flower I asked for?" Later, we drove down to the bay and wandered through the driftwood. There was no one else around. I looked down, and leaning against a log was a small bouquet of flowers. I laughed and said, "Thank you, Azna. I asked for a flower, and I got a whole bouquet!"

෴ ෴ ෴

Linda writes:

There was a time when I was having panic attacks. I don't know if that's what they really were, but that's what I call them. I've loved Sylvia from the moment I first read her words, and have learned so much from her work. I place absolute trust in her and have delved into her books with complete trust that I would be able to somehow overcome this.

She spoke about calling on Azna and petitioning Her and asking for a sign. When I first started this process, I dreamt that I was at work, typing along, when a sign popped up telling me I had a message. I tried and tried to retrieve my message but couldn't figure out how to get it. The sign I asked for from Mother God was to bring me a flower, just as Sylvia advised, and I placed a time frame on it, as Sylvia said: within seven days.

The sign came to me so quickly, and I was so overwhelmed with Mother Azna's love. I literally felt Her arms around me when I saw the flower on my computer the next day at work, and a feeling of peace came over me so quickly. I can't remember Sylvia's words exactly, but they were something to the effect that She waits for us so *patiently. Now, whenever I'm in that situation, I breathe deeply and calmly and feel Her overpowering love for me. It makes me love others as well. I thank you, Mother. And I thank you, Sylvia.*

❧❧❧ ❧❧❧ ❧❧❧

This next letter is from Tom, who pretty much says it all when he states that his life is easier with Azna in it. He writes:

I've become so accustomed to petitions to Azna being answered that it's hard for me now to think of one particular event that illustrates Her awesome compassion and love. But I can say with honesty that my life has become so much easier in so many small ways that I don't know how I survived life without Her interventions before I turned to Her. Whenever I find myself facing an emotionally difficult task, or one of life's countless curve balls, I always ask Her to intervene so that I get through it as easily as possible. As a result, life no longer seems as challenging as it once was.

≈◊❧ ≈◊❧ ≈◊❧

There doesn't seem to be any area that Azna can't address. She seems to care about all facets of human nature that cause Her children pain. True, some people call on Her when they're at the end of their proverbial rope, but She also answers simpler petitions—like helping someone catch a plane on time, find lost items, or care for sick pets. The following letter shows how Mother God answers prayers, even about finances.

Angelina writes:

My husband had lost his job, and I was having a very hard time. I'm a great believer in Azna, and I do trust in Her and love Her with all my heart. On one of my worst days, I asked Her, "Are you listening to me, Mother? I'm hurting and feel lost. If you're there, please send me a sign that everything will be okay. The sign will

*be a rose that will be given to me by any-
one you choose."*

*Within one week, my sister gave me a
small gift, a decoration for my home—a
box containing a purse and a pair of shoes,
with pink roses on both. I keep them in
front of my door so I'll never forget Azna's
promise that everything will be all right
and that She does listen. My husband has
a job today, just as Azna promised. I'm
also happy She chose my sister to deliver
the roses, for she means a lot to me.*

⁂⁂⁂

The letters that I've gotten from the youth of
America are mind-boggling and gratifying. They tell
me that, because of Azna, they've removed themselves from gangs, drugs, alcohol, and all the things
that plague this generation.

This next letter from a young man named Paul
shows that it often takes time for prayers to be
answered, but if you continue like he did, you'll
become stronger and gain greater insight. And if
you're the parent of a teenager or a young child in

pain, petition Azna on their behalf. After all, She is your Mother.

Paul writes:

Four years ago when I started high school, I endured the worst treatment you could ever imagine. People made fun of me, and I used to come home and cry hysterically every night. I was suicidal during that time period. I planned to kill myself, including the ways to do it. I used to pray and cry to Azna every night, wishing I would never wake up, pleading and begging Her to cut my life short, to take me now.

I tried so hard to escape the inevitable, yet each and every day I woke up and suffered inhumane abuse that no one should ever endure. And why? Because of people's inability to see who I really was and am, instead of taking everything at face value. The way I looked and acted wasn't truly me nor will it ever be what I represent. And how could it have been my fault that they couldn't see through that, to see something more than a "loser," nothing more than a "nerd"? The other kids used to tease me and make fun of me so much that their repetitiveness complicated my truths and distorted what was real from what wasn't real, to the point that I began to believe what they said about me.

Do I blame Azna and God for what I endured? Of course not. It may have taken a year, but I got through it and became stronger than before, stronger than I ever thought I could be. I thank Azna with all my heart and soul for getting me through those very rough times, for listening to my pleas and prayers of desperation for more than a year, and for understanding where I was coming from. This might have impacted my immense belief and protectiveness of my religion and Azna. What I needed during those lonely nights was a loving, understanding God, not a vengeful and mean God. God alone was the only One who could have helped me, and She did.

As I cried and pleaded each night, I didn't know if anybody was listening. I *felt so stranded and so lonely. I didn't know if Azna truly did exist, because She seemed like She didn't. Never an answer or sign did I receive. When it was all said and done, this is why my faith in Her diminished, and this is why my truth and knowledge in Azna resurrected. This is why, without a doubt in my mind, Azna does in fact exist. Because how I got through that rough time can only have manifested due to a very high source: Azna. That depression was the worst and probably the first. I truly did hit bottom. And that's why I'm so defensive when it comes to Azna and God, because without Her, I would never have made it, and I say that without a shadow of a doubt.*

꩜ ꩜ ꩜

From jewelry to keys to even more serious life-and-death problems, there really doesn't seem to be anything too small or too large for Azna to answer.

Dawn writes:

I have a story of a granted petition from Azna. I was shopping one day with my twin sons and nephew, and when it was time to check out and go to the car, I noticed that I didn't have my keys. I was starting to freak. I went to the car and there they were, hanging in the ignition. Did I panic! I had three kids and a cart full of perishable items. I called my insurance company—no answer. I called every locksmith, but no one could come right away except for one lady. When she arrived, I didn't think she knew what she was doing. A half hour passed and she couldn't get my doors open. By this time, my twins had worn my patience out. (They're what I call twin terrors—God bless them, though.) Then I remembered that if I prayed to Azna, She would help. I prayed really hard for Azna to send angels to help. I begged. It was about three minutes, when out of nowhere came a cable guy. It took him about ten minutes and my doors were opened. It could've all been a coincidence, but I'd rather think it was my Mother answering my call.

❧ ❧ ❧

Real estate salespeople could take a lesson from Janet. She writes:

This was my most recent request to Mother Azna.

My husband and I are in the process of separating, and I'm the one who's moving out. With my two cats, renting is almost not an option, and there are very few homes in my price range in New Jersey (where I'm from and want to continue living). So my request to Azna had some very specific requirements for a real estate purchase. Equal in importance were price and an absolutely safe area away from traffic for my cats. (I've lived in rural suburbia on the edge of the woods, in three other homes, for about 15 years.) I like an open floor plan for my main living space as opposed to separate rooms. Also, I need easy access because my mother doesn't do well on stairs anymore.

After searching the multiple listings online for a couple of weeks, doing "drive-bys" for locations, and finally looking at one condo at the high end of my price range that I didn't like anyway, I reluctantly went to see what I thought was going to be a tiny little condo with tiny little closets. When I walked in, my first reaction was "Ooooh!" It was located in a ski resort area, slope side, with NO traffic. It had a few very shallow stairs (in an area where most of the units have full staircases if not two), and it was on the last tier up, with no other units behind it. It offered sunset views, a wide-open floor plan, a large kitchen, good appliances, newer carpet and tile, and it was well within my price range. At a time when bidding wars were going on in New Jersey, I got it for less than the list price. (The closets are small, but I'm trying to downsize anyway.) I just kept on saying, "Thank you, thank you" all the way home.

I close in a month and a half, and I'm so excited. Looking back, this is just the latest of my many homes from Azna.

❧❧ ❧❧ ❧❧

Although the next letter is short, its message is nevertheless very poignant in describing the help the writer received from Azna. Sue writes:

After the death of my sister, life as I knew it was different. My niece came to live with me and had a terrible time getting over the death of her mother. I prayed to Azna for relief for her and guidance for me, and shortly after, the weight was lifted. Thank you, Sylvia, for all your books. They prepared me for a very difficult time in my life.

❧❧ ❧❧ ❧❧

As this next writer says, we are all messengers. If I am, so are you. Gayle writes:

> *I really hope to meet Sylvia one day in this life, as I admire her so much. I lived in San Jose for 30 years, and I wish I'd known about her and Novus Spiritus then. I've been in North Carolina for almost three years. I'm going to visit Novus Spiritus when I visit the Bay Area in July. Please tell Sylvia I am forever grateful to her for writing her books and telling the world the truth about why we are here on Earth, and the paradise that awaits those of us who are from the light side. I try to be as nice as I can to people and help everyone who wants me to help them. I am Mother and Father God's messenger.*

aᴼᵥ aᴼᵥ aᴼᵥ

As I looked over the literally hundreds of letters, I tried to find a category Azna hadn't addressed, but there just wasn't one. No matter how small or large the request, or how often you keep asking, an all-perfect God cannot and will not get aggravated, impatient, or disgusted with your petitions.

Vickie writes:

Over the past couple of years, my family has endured many hardships, including the deaths of three close family members. I was laid off from my job and, being a single parent raising three kids, life became very difficult—especially since their father had been killed by a drunk driver. But what made things even worse was that their wealthy and influential aunt sued me for custody of my two youngest children.

This is a case that should never have been heard in court, but in a small town where everyone knows everyone, the judge agreed to hear it. After hearing the aunt testify and refusing to hear me, he gave her custody. I was devastated and quickly became depressed. I was always used to my house being full of my kids and their friends, and now my home was down to one child (whom the aunt didn't want).

I'd started reading Sylvia's books when my sister died of cancer last year. You have no idea how much hope Sylvia's words restored back into my life. About six weeks after the children left to go live with their aunt, I couldn't handle it anymore. I couldn't eat or sleep, and all I could do was cry. Then I bought Sylvia's book God, Creation, and Tools for Life. *One evening I ran across the section where it says that if you're going through something that's too much for you to handle, you can petition Mother Azna for help and She can bring you through it quickly. I did exactly what Sylvia said to do, and I'm here to tell you that it didn't take any attorneys or any appeals court. My daughter returned home within 14 days of my petitioning Mother Azna. My son has to finish out the school year, then he'll be home at the end of May.*

I've always been a spirit-filled Christian and would never believe the things Sylvia says in her books if I hadn't experienced so much of it firsthand. Thanks for everything, and may God bless your ministry.

I think it's good to ask, as Vickie did, for your petition to be granted as quickly as possible, to put you out of your misery. When I ask Azna for help, I often say "now," or maybe "by the end of the month."

Very recently, a friend whom I'm now dating and I were meeting my oldest son and his significant other for dinner. The restaurant was outdoors, at a resort. We arrived first and were seated near a table of 10 or 12 very drunk guys who were beginning to be very rowdy and crude. "Please, Azna," I said, "take them away to another table so my son doesn't hear their crudeness and decide to defend his mother." In the twinkling of an eye, as they say, one guy got up and said, "Let's blow this joint and find some action." They left, and along came my son. I said, "Thank you, Azna."

I also say it every time payroll period rolls around (yes, people think I'm so rich). I petition Azna for enough money to pay my staff and all the people who help me. It takes a lot to run a large organization, and every month Linda (our payroll clerk) says, "Yeah! We just made it! Thank you, Azna."

This next letter from Betty is beautiful. It not only tells about prayers being answered, it also talks about gratitude, which we so often forget. Not that Mother God needs it, but we need to learn to be grateful for all the miracles life gives us.

Betty writes:

A year ago, out of the blue, my daughter had pain in her ten fingertips, and we rushed to the doctor (it turned out to be seven doctors). My daughter had all kinds of tests done, but the pain was still there.

Some of the doctors didn't seem to believe her, but she'd tell me that her fingers were on fire. And, yes, I did see some kind of blisters on the fingertips, but not on the outside; it was strange. The burning was inside the skin, not on the outside, and once I even saw a circle (like chicken pox with pus). The following day we rushed to the dermatologist, but there was nothing on the tips (only the pain), and we went home. I cried. Then I started speaking to God like I always do, but this time, out of the blue, I remembered reading about the

*beautiful Mother Azna in one of Sylvia's
books, and boy, did I talk and pray to Her.*

*Meanwhile, the company I work for
voted for a strike, and it was a very difficult time. I was scared, but my prayers
were answered. Just like that, my daughter
came up to me and said, "Mom, there's no
more pain," and I didn't have to worry
about the money either. I was talking to the
Beautiful Lady about that, too (since I have
no insurance), and wouldn't you know that
the strike lasted about a month. I've always
had the Beautiful Lady in my heart. Now
that I think about it, I would always pray
to Her for world peace (She's holding the
world in Her hands) when I was a kid,
and I always buy flowers to say "thank
you"—She knows that.*

*I have asked for signs from Her in
roses, and yes, they do come. When it happens, it's like my heart is being hugged.
It's incredible; the feeling is hard to
describe. I guess because of society, I
always prayed to Her for other people.
Then I remembered what Sylvia wrote in*

her book: Azna is here for us (for me!), and She came through. I know now, this very minute, that all these years, it's been Azna. Wow! And I know not to fool around with Her—She means business.

In April, it will be a year since my daughter was sick. I love Azna for life, not only for that, but for everything else that She is doing. Maybe one day I'll ask to see Her.

P.S.: The roses do come from Her as a sign. She's listening.

❧❧ ❧❧ ❧❧

The next story is poignant and somewhat humorous, but also proves that nothing is too insignificant for Azna to address.

Mary Lou writes:

It seems strange to be telling this story to someone I haven't met, especially since the few friends that I've discussed it with have looked at me as though I've lost touch with reality.

My daughter was working in China recently and needed to come home without fulfilling her contract. I won't go into the details, but suffice it to say that some of us here were concerned for her safety. At about the time she was getting ready to begin her "escape," I was awake and anxious. I have a heart condition, and my heart was beating irregularly. I had been reading Sylvia's books and decided that I would try praying to Azna. Just before praying, I'd been tending to a small terrarium in which I had a small black widow spider. I talked to the spider and bemoaned the fact that she was so tiny when I would love to have a large specimen. Then I prayed to Mother Azna.

I prayed for the safety of my beautiful daughter and asked that Azna take a personal interest and make everything easy. I knew that there were likely to be problems with a locked door where Esther must leave a key and message, and that she might be seen or stopped at the airport for not having the right exit permit. So I prayed and then I asked that, if Azna wouldn't mind, I'd like a sign so I'd know that all was indeed going to be well, that I'd know Azna had heard my prayer, and that She was going to take things into Her hands. Then I'd be able to rest and not be worried.

I ended my prayer and realized that I might not recognize the sign. I need not have worried. I went into my bedroom to get the medications that were due, and there, right beside my pill case, was the largest, most beautiful black widow spider I've ever seen. I couldn't believe my eyes. I laughed and spoke out loud, telling Mother Azna that she has a wicked sense of humor. I captured the spider and placed her in the terrarium, where she remains as a reminder of my Mother's love. You might think this a coincidence, but I cannot. I've never seen this species of spider in the house before, and why at that particular moment? It was the perfect sign to give me

And yes, my daughter was amazed at how things went for her. A door that was always locked was not only unlocked, but

*propped open when she got there. At the
airport, they noticed the missing permit
but let her continue when she got tears in
her eyes and said she needed to go home.*

*I've had many wonderful spiritual
experiences in my lifetime. I've been searching all my life for the truth, and I believe
I've found it in Sylvia's books.*

≈☙ ≈☙ ≈☙

This next letter from Debbie shows how, even
in the darkest of times, Azna comes to us. She
writes:

*I'm married with two children, and liv-
ing in Arizona. I moved here six years ago,
had a hard time coping with my homesick
feelings, and made life miserable for my
husband. I was also pregnant at the time,
so my emotions were out of control.*

*Recently I went home to Georgia for a
visit by myself. My mom came in to help
my husband take care of my kids while I
was away. I came back totally wrecked*

about being so far away from my friends and loved ones. On top of that, I realized how overbearing my mom and husband were, and all I could think of was running away from my pain. I was miserable and angry at God and the Council for letting me choose this option.

I'd scheduled a reading from Sylvia months before this and wasn't even supposed to be called for a reading date for at least five more months. (They said it would be a year and a half on the waiting list.) After my first night home from my trip—in just a horrible state of mind—I pleaded with Azna for help. I just knew that if someone didn't do something fast to spare me of this hopeless pain, I was going to die.

A couple of days later, I received a call from Sylvia's office. They were ready to make my appointment, and it was only going to be a month away. I know Azna answered my request, I know She sent me help, and I know that She exists! I wish everyone knew.

This may not seem like a very important request, but to me it was a lifesaver.

∂☙ ∂☙ ∂☙

Two short letters from Claudia and Pam also show that She immediately answers. Claudia writes:

My sister had been trying to get pregnant for about ten years. I told her what I'd read about Mother God, Azna, from your books, and I told her she should petition Azna about getting pregnant (basically to put Her power to the test).

Well, my sister did just as I told her, and she became a happy new mom to a baby girl named Peaches, born on St. Patrick's Day.

∂☙ ∂☙ ∂☙

Pam writes:

I recently had to give a presentation at work in front of management about an error in my work. I was terrified. I prayed to Azna for help. I was shaking until I stood up in front of them. I was suddenly fine, spoke intelligently, and got through it. I attribute the help to Her.

〰 〰 〰

Contrary to what this next letter-writer thinks, the following letter is not corny at all. It shows that in all human endeavor or circumstances—big, small, sad, tragic, or fearful—nothing is beyond Azna's realm.

Shannon writes:

I know this may sound sort of corny, but I thought I'd share it anyway. I have an old Dodge Caravan that isn't currently running. The driver's-side window got busted out when my husband was attempting to fix it one day, and I really wanted to get it fixed and running.

One week, it started raining, and the forecast said it would rain for several more days. I'd forgotten to cover the window so that the inside of the van wouldn't get totally drenched, and by the time I remembered to do so, I figured it was too late anyway. I prayed to Azna about it. I said, "Dear Azna, I love the rain, but could you please make sure the inside of the van doesn't get ruined because of it?" I continued to pray about this every day until the rain stopped. Then when the rain finally did stop, I went out to the van, opened the door with the broken window, and felt around the inside of that area. It was bone dry! Not even a little damp! It was as if Azna had placed a protective covering over the window area so that no rain could get in at all.

I was so incredibly happy. To this day, I continually thank Azna for all of the *precious, wonderful things She does for me—and for everybody, for that matter.*

ᕦᕧ ᕦᕧ ᕦᕧ

Every one of these letters, as I've said before, was more than heartwarming. They could be classified (and I don't hesitate to say it in this day of technical analysis) as nothing short of miraculous. Humans have always had a bit of a problem with the word *miracles,* preferring instead to call things "circumstances" or "coincidences," but when you begin to stack up the thousands of incidents, big and small, they give you great cause for pause. Even the greatest skeptic would have to admit that miracles could possibly exist.

∾∾ ∾∾ ∾∾ ∾∾ ∾∾

Chapter Six

PRAYERS AND
MEDITATIONS

P lease don't ever neglect our Father, Christ, and the Holy Spirit, but when you want to call on Mother God, here are some prayers and meditations that have helped me and others. Or you certainly can make up your own. After all, She is the Mother of us all and has the heart of a loving mother, too.

Prayers

Dearest Mother,

Please know my heartfelt thoughts, and also come into my heart and soul. Make yourself known to me, not only through my petitions, but fill me with your grace and knowledge. Walk with your mantle of protection around not only me, but all my loved ones. In this time of strife, keep your protection around the world so we can have peace and prosperity.

I petition you to help the sick, the frail, the poor, the dying, and those in despair. Help me also to assist all those in need, and give me the strength of your mighty sword to cut down darkness and adversity. Bring love, prosperity, health, and harmony to my home and family. I know I must learn my lessons, but as a mother soothes the wounds of a child, hold me tightly and absorb my pain.

Loving Mother, I stand as witness to your power and accept your unconditional love.

Amen.

෴෴෴

Dearest Queen of the Universe,

Attend me this day. Put your silver pearl net around my enemies, and surround me with your golden light. Let depression and negativity be taken from me so that my light can shine as an example for others. Let your Thrones, your special angels, attend me. Use your sword to cut away all pain and suffering from my life. I never ask that you use your sword for good, for I know that that is your only purpose, but I never want to use or ask for your power to hurt or harm, because I know that then my petition will be negated.

I ask that I be kept on my charted path and that you walk with me every step of my journey in this life, until I can be reunited with you in the gigantic rose garden on the Other Side, where your beautiful statue stands.

I want to stand witness to your imminent incarnation and to the fact that you always were and always will be for the world, and that with your maternal love, you will bring love and peace to all people.

Amen.

ᴬᎧᵥ ᴬᎧᵥ ᴬᎧᵥ

Meditations

Lie in a quiet place or sit in a comfortable chair. Begin to relax your feet, your calves, your thighs, your whole buttocks area, and all through the trunk of your body, and relax all the organs therein.

Move a golden healing light through your whole body, even up through your neck and down your shoulders, upper arms, hands, and fingertips. From the top of your head to your toes, let Mother God's golden light infuse you, and let the power of created magnificence and protection come into your heart, mind, body, and soul.

Say to yourself:

Dear Azna, help me clear any obstacles in my path that I have written in my chart. If I am meant to go through them, help me have the strength to go through them with love, hope, and dignity. Never let go of my hand. Bring the hosts of heaven with you and God the Father, Son, and Holy Spirit. Attend me now in my hour of need. I ask for relief immediately from physical or mental illness for me or a loved one [name them]. *Send your love and help also to all those who need you. At my hour of death, let me just step over the threshold easily and be with you and my Divine Father and all my loved ones.*

Now ask that energy come up through your feet, calves, thighs, trunk, neck, shoulders, arms, and head, and ask that you will come out feeling better than you ever have.

One, two, three . . . come up to complete consciousness.

≈◎ ≈◎ ≈◎

Lie in a prone position or sit comfortably. Relax all parts of your body, beginning with your feet, and go through to the top of your head.

With your body completely relaxed, visualize yourself outside of your body. There, standing in front of you in all Her magnificence, is Mother God, dressed in silver and gold. She has magnificent, luminous eyes that seem to see right through you, but with love, forgiveness, and understanding. You reach for Her hand, and as She gently pulls you, you feel yourself being lifted and floating. You float through beautiful rainbow-colored mists. Each color seeps into one of your chakras (the physical or spiritual energy centers in your body that correspond to the major nerve centers, or plexuses, located along your spinal column). Green goes through your body to heal. Gold gives you hope and belief. Purple gives you higher spirituality. Pink gives you love. Blue gives you peace. Orange is for higher learning. White is for purity and protection.

Try to go to the rose garden with Mother God. See the colors, and smell the heady aroma of all the roses that fill the air. Stay with Her for a while and put in any petitions you may have by speaking with Her. Use Her now to visit a friend or loved one who needs help, maybe someone you're not even aware of who needs assistance with life. Also petition Her for help with your life and your growing spirituality so you can stay on course.

Feel yourself being pulled back to yourself. You can take this journey as many times as you want. Each time it gets stronger, and soon you'll be able to get out of your body and even visit the Other Side. Pull yourself back to complete consciousness . . . one, two, three.

Please note: Do not use red as a rainbow color in your meditation, for it's an angry color. Also, write down two copies of your petition, either before or after your meditation. Burn one copy of the petition in offering it to Mother God. Save the other copy and look at it six months or a year later. You'll be surprised at how many requests were granted.

~~~ ~~~ ~~~ ~~~ ~~~

Afterword

If you've gotten this far and have opened yourself up to the possibility of a duality of creation, I'm glad; but if not, then that's fine, also, because each one of you must find your own role in life and your own path.

I just ask, as I always have, that you continue to seek out and thank God. As Christ said, "Seek and ye shall find." Even on the Other Side, we keep searching and seeking and knocking so truth will open the door.

I personally couldn't think of a life without Mother God, and all who have embraced Her will tell you the same thing. So if nothing else, whether because of your desire for valid testing or your own skepticism, try calling on Her for love and support. You'll find that it works—that I'm assured of. But regardless, as Tiny Tim said in Charles Dickens's *A Christmas Carol:* "God bless us every one."

God love you. I do.

— **Sylvia**

ABOUT THE AUTHOR

Millions of people have witnessed **Sylvia Browne's** incredible psychic powers on TV shows such as *Montel, Larry King Live, Entertainment Tonight,* and *Unsolved Mysteries;* and she has been profiled in *Cosmopolitan, People* magazine, and other national media. Sylvia is the author of numerous books and audios; is the president of the Sylvia Browne Corporation; and is the founder of her church, the Society of Novus Spiritus, located in Campbell, California. Please contact Sylvia at: **www.sylvia.org,** or call **(408) 379-7070** for further information about her work.

~~ ~~ ~~ ~~ ~~

About the Artist

Christina Simonds is on the staff at Sylvia Browne's office, and is an ordained minister of the Society of Novus Spiritus. She's an illustrator who sees her work as a means to convey the Gnostic Christian philosophy through symbolism within her art. To purchase reprints of the drawings in this book, please visit her Website at: **www.angelart-cs.com.**

∿∿ ∿∿ ∿∿ ∿∿ ∿∿

Hay House Titles of Related Interest

Books

Archangels & Ascended Masters,
by Doreen Virtue, Ph.D.

The God Code, by Gregg Braden

Holy Spirit for Healing, by Ron Roth, Ph.D.,
with Peter Occhiogrosso

The Jesus Code, by John Randolph Price

The Power of Intention, by Dr. Wayne W. Dyer

Prayer and the Five Stages of Healing,
by Ron Roth, Ph.D., with Peter Occhiogrosso

Card Decks

Comfort Cards, by Max Lucado

Healing with the Angels Oracle Cards,
by Doreen Virtue, Ph.D.

The Prayer of Jabez™ Cards (and *The Prayer of
Jabez™ Cards for Teens),* by Bruce Wilkinson

Secrets of the Vine™ Cards, by Bruce Wilkinson

All of the above are available at your local
bookstore, or may be ordered by visiting:
Hay House USA: **www.hayhouse.com**
Hay House Australia: **www.hayhouse.com.au**
Hay House UK: **www.hayhouse.co.uk**
Hay House South Africa: **orders@psdprom.co.za**

æØv æØv æØv

✺✹ ✺✹ ✺✹

A note from the author: You might want to use the following "Notes" pages to petition Mother God or make personal observations. All the best to you!

— Sylvia

✺✹ ✺✹ ✺✹

NOTES